Gems

Bernhard Graf

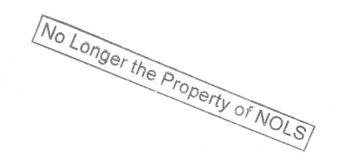

Gems

The World's Greatest Treasures and their Stories

Prestel

Munich · London · New York

Table of Contents

Foreword

The human body like a rusty ship
With priceless gemstones filling it
Sapphires, emeralds and aquamarine,
Diamonds, rubies—all stones.

Transient the body, shadows in the dark,
Inner purity, higher goals to embark,
Where God lives among his own,
Sleeping hidden on a bed of precious stone.

After a poem in the southeast Indian Telugu language

The desire for precious stones and minerals is as old as humankind. In India, China, America, Europe and all the world over, people equate what they love most – their most precious values, their immortal soul, their deities – with gems. They esteem diamonds, sapphires and emeralds and accord them a value beyond worldly wealth. Just one gemstone is enough to contemplate all of nature. The Roman scholar Pliny the Elder also shared this belief. He related the idea with the story of Prometheus, the Greek mythical figure, when he compared the Caucasian cliff to which Prometheus' brother Atlas was chained to a precious stone.

Since the Stone Age the interest in rare, perfect and costly minerals has grown along with man's need to find his own limitations and emphasize his own importance. This fascination has not changed to this day. Esoteric literature about gems is more popular than ever. Our high-tech, industrialized society yearns for the inner strength and peace found in nature and, above all, in gems. The growing demand for products from nature has also resulted in the production of an endless variety of articles made of minerals. Consider just a few more to their roots, based on the thousands-of-years-old practice of lithotherapy.

Theories which until recently lacked a firm scientific basis have now been confirmed by scientific research in microbiology and biophysics. Researchers at European and American universities of mineralogy and crystallography are constantly working to discover new minerals, scrutinize their properties and track down their interaction with their environment. The demand for books about mineralogy, therefore, is also increasing both among the general public and in the industrial sector.

In the manufacturing of micro-chips and the discovery of alternative sources of energy, it is no longer possible to ignore minerals and synthetic crystals. This book places less emphasis on present-day technological and medical applications of minerals, their cult value and their esoteric associations. Rather, it emphasizes details drawn from history, art and art history which books on

The Regent, a 140.5-carat Indian diamond found by a slave in the 18th century, had a chequered history before finishing up on Napoleon's sword (seen here with its owner). It is now the most famous diamond in French history.

minerals have until now neglected. This book is, among other things, about the significance of jewels in works of art, about minerals that are used as paint pigments and polishing compounds, about the magic and healing power of gems which historic figures strongly believed in and about the important gems which rulers, religious leaders, scholars and simple people had and entrusted.

Art objects from nearly all the world's cultures have been selected in order to focus on the magic of gems. So the reader encounters many historically famous figures from a new and previously unknown perspective; for example: the Egyptian pharaoh Tutankhamun, the biblical fathers Moses and Aaron, the Chinese philosopher Confucius, the Greek philosopher Plato, Pope Gregory the Great, the Prophet Mohammed, the Arabian physician Avicenna, the historical poet Chrétien de Troyes, the conquistador Hernando Cortés, the Spanish mystic Theresa of Avila, the royal mistress Diane de Potiers, Indian moguls, the English discoverer Captain James Cook, Emperor Napoleon I, the American author Edgar Allan Poe, or Chilean poet (and diplomat) Pablo Neruda.

Bernhard Graf

Munich, July 2001

The hilt of Napoleon's sword with the Regent diamond. Nowadays the diamond is an important exhibit in its own right.

Jade is Beauty in Stone

The culture of jade in the Far East

"Jade is beauty in stone with five virtues: its warm glow stands for humanity, its immaculate purity for moral integrity, its pleasant tone for wisdom, its hardness for justice, and its durability for steadfastness and courage."

Xu Shen, *Shuowen jiezi*, 2nd century AD

When Xu Shen expressed his admiration for the extraordinary qualities of jade in his encyclopaedia, *Shuowen jiezi*, in the second century AD, the culture of this stone had been in existence for over 8,000 years. 'Jade-face' was the term the Chinese used to praise a woman's beauty. 'Jade-heart' meant a heart that had integrity. Jade was thought to possess the essence of the strength of mountains and to be the way to the gods.

In the era of the mythical cultural hero Shennong, who lived in China around 3500 BC, jade pendants shaped like dragons embodied the unassailable, heaven-sent power of the rulers. The Niuheliang jade dragons of the northern Chinese Hongshan culture are examples. According to traditional Chinese medicine, Shennong discovered how to use plants and stones for healing. On bas-reliefs sculpted by his followers he is often depicted scraping stones. He used the powder obtained by this method as a mineral remedy. This marks the beginning of the Far Eastern science of lithotherapy.

In the 17th century BC, a ruler by the name of Tang founded the Shang dynasty, which took over the culture of jade from the Xia court. Fu Hao in particular, the wife of the 23rd king of the Shang, worshipped the gods with her pieces of jade jewellery. The Shang rulers believed that gold had an 'established value'. The value of jade, however, was 'inestimable'. Hence they set up the Yofu, a jade office at court to control trade along the jade routes between the distant West and central China. They also regulated the cutting of stones for lucky jade amulets, jade musical instruments and jade weapons, whose magical powers were relied on both in this life and the hereafter. In the late Shang Period (13th–10th century BC), jade sceptres were not only used to signal commands in battle but also placed in the hands of the dead as symbols of power.

After the decline of the Shang dynasty, the culture of jade continued under the succeeding Western Zhou (11th–7th century BC). Jade pectorals were extremely popular at court. Those in Pingdingshan in the province of Henan, for example, featured jade, agate and turquoise chains attached with serpentine dragons to a trapezoidal jade plate. The aristocratic wearer was presumably to

Jade statue of a kneeling man, from the Zhanguo (Warring States) era (481–222 BC), Eastern Zhou period. Luoyang Municipal Museum, Henan Province

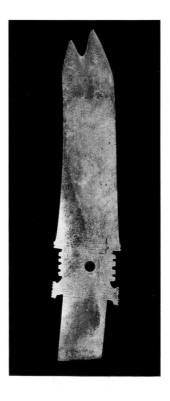

Shu culture jade sceptre from Sanxingdui, Sichuan Province. Late Shang period (15th–10th century BC). Institute of Archaeology and Culture, Sichuan Province

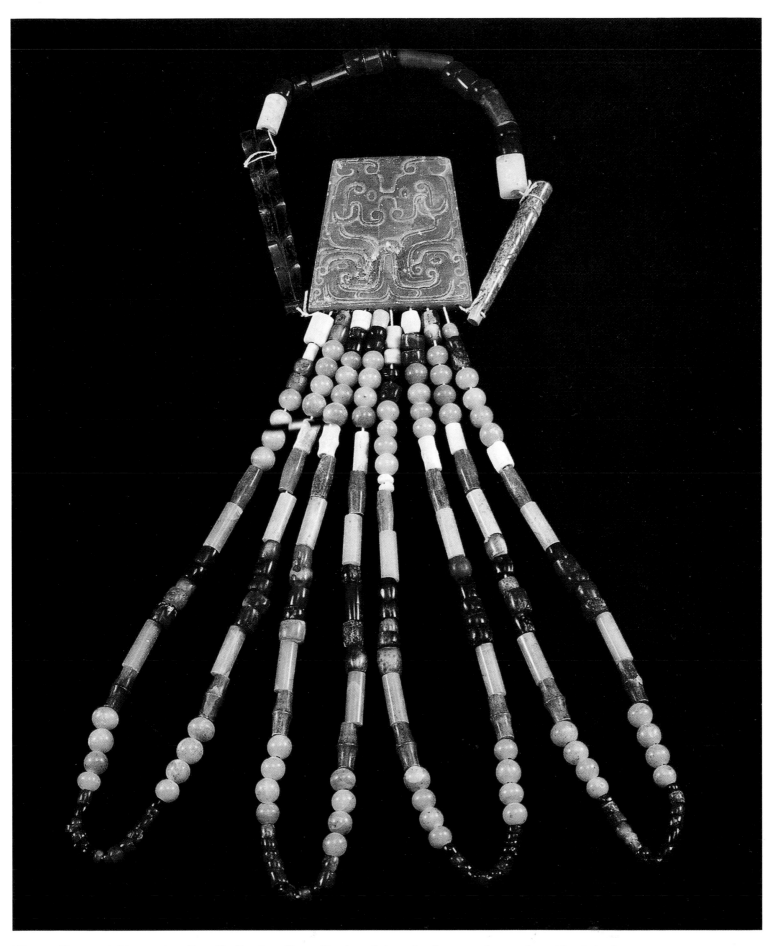

Western Zhou period breastpiece from Pindingshan, Henan Province. It is made of agate and turquoise, with a jade plaque.
Institute of Archaeology and Culture, Henan Province

The Chinese philosopher Confucius (551–479 BC)

rejected jade as a sheer luxury of the feudal upper class, Han Feizi's verdict is based on everyday life: "Gold or jade vessels, be they ever so precious, are fit for nothing when they leak, for who could use them for anything?" Confucius, on the other hand, regarded jade as an important ritual material. As he put it in the *Book of Songs*, the processing of jade is a counterpart of the human process of reaching maturity: "Ivory and precious stone first need to be cut, then polished, first filed and then smoothed." His students further elaborated his ideas. Thus developed the unique system of ritual jade to substantiate the hierarchical structure of feudal society; the king was assigned the *gui* jades named *zhen*; the five classes of the nobility the stones called *huan*, *xin*, *gong*, *gu,* and *pu.* The *Liji,* a Confucian classic, explains the jade ideal: "When the sages of old were indifferent to alabaster while jade meant so much to them, this had nothing to do with the commonness or rarity of alabaster or jade but was based on the fact that the sages compared their virtues to jade. It stands for goodness, knowledge, righteousness, decency, loyalty and confidence."

In 221 BC, Quin Shihuang, the first Emperor of China, unified the scattered empire and founded his own dynasty. Only nineteen years later it was superseded by the Han dynasty under Emperor Liu Bang. Under his successors Confucianism become the leading philosophy of the empire. In Emperor Wu's reign (140–87 BC) the jade code dominated court ceremonial, with *gui* jades indicating class distinctions, ritual jades as religious accessories, jade charms to protect the wearer and impressive burial

be protected against evil forces. This would correspond to medical practices during the Chu Empire (extending all the way to south Henan around 700 BC) which used jade amulets, talismans and seals to banish misfortune caused by demons.

During the Warring States Period of Huang, Fu, Zhong-shan and Zeng (770–221 BC), Chinese artisans made the grinding wheels more efficient by increasing the number of revolutions and adding corundum sand. This abrasive, made from rubies and sapphires, had a considerably higher hardness than jade on the Mohs scale.

Contemporary schools of philosophy had quite divergent views on the culture of jade. While Mozi utterly

Fifteen-part 'face-guard' for a dead man (length 2-6 cm), Zhanguo (Warring States) era of Eastern Zhou period (481–222 BC). Luoyang Municipal Musuem, Henan Province

Prince Liu Sheng's jade helmet, with *bi* disc, Western Han period (c. 113 BC). Hebei Provincial Museum

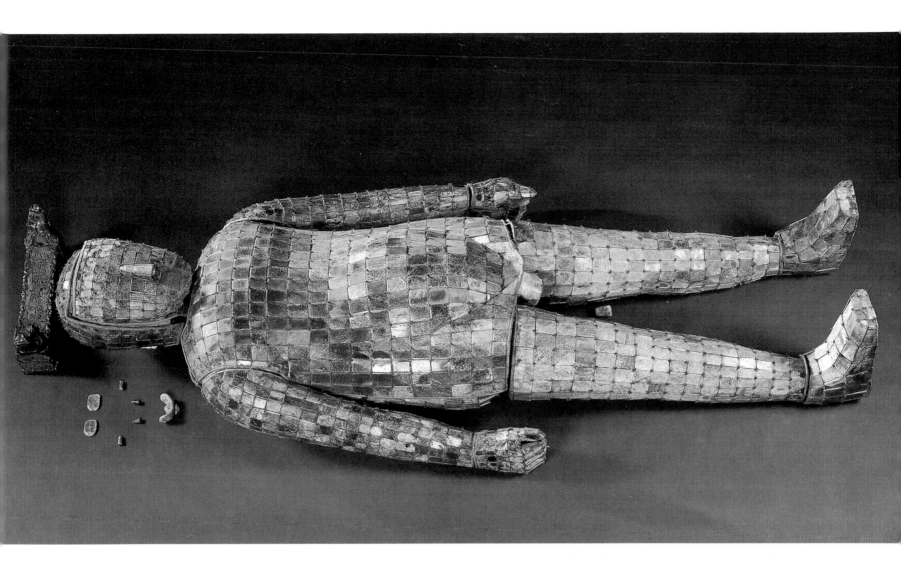

Prince Liu Sheng's death suit or shroud, Western Han period (c. 113 BC). It is made of jade tiles, and beside a headrest has nine jade orifice plugs. According to contemporary beliefs, these prevented decay. Hebei Provincial Museum

jades. Liu Sheng, Prince of Zhongshan, was buried with numerous jades in about 113 BC, as was the Han Emperor Wu later. These included nine jade seals for body orifices, placed on the ruler's eyes, ears, nostrils, mouth, anus and genitals. According to Ge Hong (284–363 AD), they were to prevent the decomposition of the corpse. In addition, Liu Sheng's shroud was a suit of jade plate and his head-rest was also made of jade. The magical powers of the stone were to equip him for immortality after a lifetime in which he had 'loved wine and women'. This privilege was reserved solely for the rulers of the Han dynasty, their family and exceptionally deserving subjects.

Although the teachings of Confucius became modified in subsequent empires and merged with Buddhist teachings during the Sui (581–618 AD) and Tang dynasties (618–907 AD), the Chinese culture of jade lived on in the form of jade figures of Buddha. The ceremonial jade system, however, was forgotten. Thus Johannes Grueber, an Austrian Jesuit on a papal mission, observed a different code when he visited the Manchu emperors Shun-Chih (1644–1661) and K'ang-hsi (1662–1722): "The great lords wear various precious stones. Several also wear a pearl, but in combination with a ruby, emerald or jasper bead for, as we have heard, only the ruler is allowed to wear a single pearl on his headdress."

Almost Beyond the Reach of the Gods

The spell of Indian precious stones and minerals

"The ruby is the lord of the daytime …
The emerald the stone of noble Mercury,
The yellow sapphire the precious stone of Jupiter,
*   the teacher of the gods,*
The diamond is that of Venus, the teacher of the demons,
The blue sapphire that of Saturn,
The hyacinth that of Rahu,
And the cat's-eye that of Kethu."

Jatak Parijat, Vedic astrology book, 1300–1000 BC

Tassels of pearls and a diamond necklet feature prominently in this portrait of Maharaja Sayajee Rao (regent of Baroda from 1875-1936) by the brilliant 19th-century Keralan painter Rajah Ravi Varma.

Travellers through the ages have always sung the praises of the immeasurable wealth of India: its prosperous stretches of countryside and its opulent cities, the magnificent palaces and temples and the thousands upon thousands of jewels in the treasuries of the grand moguls and maharajas.

Long before the Mogul emperors ruled India, the civilizations of the Indus Valley employed architects who showed an interest in minerals and gems. In their writings on geomancy, the *Vasati*, they discussed the laws of energy in space, the earth's magnetic field, the subtle energies of the planetary system and even gravity as early as 5,000 years ago. The application of these ideas to architecture involved the use of minerals and precious stones.

For palaces and temples the ancient Indian *Manasara*, a classic *Vasati* architecture manual (about 3000 BC), recommended: "Leave an opening in the middle of the column for inserting precious stones … in the hollow of the base of the column also place minerals and precious stones. Then honour the column, decorated with fabrics and garlands, with flowers and scent and make food offerings to it: 'Oh column, you mighty Mount Meru, on your peak you carry all other columns'." The Indus Civilisation also had stone cutters, who polished minerals such as steatite, agate, jasper and carnelian, to make, for instance, the necklaces found in Mohenjodaro.

The Indo-Europeans supplanting the Indus Civilisation around 1400 BC refined the ideas in the *Vasati*. They collected their knowledge in the *Veda*, comprising the wisdom of the verses (*Rig Veda*), songs (*Samaveda*), sacrificial prayers (*Yajurveda*) and of the priest Atharvan (*Atharvaveda*). In the *Rig Veda* (after 1300 BC), the oldest Indian book in Sanskrit, the priest poets refer to the power of precious stones to influence subtle energies and to connect the earth to the other planets and stars in the solar system. In the *Jatak Parijat* they even assigned precious stones to the various gods and emphasised the polarity between the planetary deities and the natural forces on earth. Based on these convictions the Vedic Indo-Europeans developed the medical teachings of *Ayurveda*. These revolve around activating the self-healing powers of the diseased body with mineral

An abundance of rubies, emeralds and diamonds on the eyes, crest, beak and feathers vie with the opulent plumage of a real peacock.

The peacock with the ruby eyes (17th century) crowned the canopy of the Maharaja of Mysore's throne. According to Indian legend, a visitor on whom the peacock's shadow fell became the successor of the reigning rajah.

Shah Jahan, builder
of the Taj Mahal.
Mogul School miniature
from *c.* 1615.
Victoria & Albert
Museum, London

powders and other natural products, thus restoring harmony between the soul, body and mind. The Indians were even able to pulverise the diamonds mined in Dekkan in southern India. The oil-bound diamond powder was sold as an abrasive as far away as Europe. Alexander the Great had opened up communication to the western world in 326 BC with the defeat of King Poros on the banks of the River Hydaspes (today's Jhelum) and the conquest of the Paurava Empire. According to the maxims on statecraft in the *Arthashastra* (1st century AD) attributed to Kautilya, a minister of the Maurya Emperor Chandragupta, there were overseers in charge of the mining, trade and processing of minerals. Information on the Indian culture of precious stones eventually spread to the Greeks and the Romans. The Greek geographer Strabo (about 63 BC–19 AD) expressed his admiration for the splendour of India's rulers in his geography book. As far as he knew they owned tables, chairs, drinking vessels and bathtubs encrusted with emeralds, beryls and carbuncle stones. They had even exported a ruby reliquary (2nd century AD) as far away as the *stupa* of Bimaran in Afghanistan. The repository of Indian knowledge on gems was the *Ratna-pariksa*, a lapidary of the 6th century AD. Mainly the poets and merchants wanting to find out about the sources, quality, powers and cost of individual minerals consulted this book. It told them, for instance, that the colour of the sapphire is like the dark blue shimmer of a lotus blossom.

The fairy-tale reputation of India lasted through the Middle Ages, substantiated by travel accounts such as *Il Milione* by the Venetian merchant Marco Polo (1254–1324/25). He reported that "King Sundara-Pandya of Malabar … wears a necklace made exclusively of precious stones: rubies, sapphires, emeralds and so on, making it truly valuable … What this king carries around in the way of gold and precious stones is worth more than a whole city could raise as ransom."

Even in the early modern era, with the invention of the 8/8 cross-section in diamond cutting (1530), India kept its leading role in diamond processing. Working with precious stones and minerals flourished especially under the maharajas of Mysore and the Mogul emperors.

On 17 June 1631 Mumtaz Mahal, the second wife of the Great Mogul Shah Jahan (reigned 1628–66), died in childbirth. Deep sorrow and tender love inspired the ruler to erect a mausoleum: the famous Taj Mahal. It was built according to the ancient *Vasati* laws of spatial energy in Agra, the capital of his kingdom. Being a lover of precious stones, such as the diamonds known as 'Grand Mogul' (280 carat) and 'Shah' (88.7 carat), he had the cenotaph and the nearby marble lattices decorated with the most valuable material he could imagine: inlaid minerals in the *Parchin kari* technique. He was hoping that the lucky and magical powers of the stones would keep him and his beloved wife together after death. As François Bernier wrote in a letter dated 1663: "Everywhere you look you see jade … jasper and other, rare, precious kinds of stones, cut, combined and inlaid in marble in a hundred different ways." However, the jewels brought Shah Jahan no luck. Not the amber from Burma, the lapis lazuli from Afghanistan, the jade from the Chinese Turkestan, nor the minerals carnelian, agate, amethyst, jasper, emerald, chaceldony or onyx from the different regions of the Indian subcontinent saved him. He was deposed in 1658 by his son Aurangzeb (reigned 1658–1707). He was not allowed to leave the Red Fort of Agra. Eight years later, following his death, he was buried next to his wife in the Taj Mahal.

Front view
of the cenotaph

Top of the cenotaph built pre-1643 by the Great Mogul Shah Jahan for his second wife Mumtaz Mahal.
It is decorated with inlays of precious and semi-precious stones. Taj Mahal, Agra

In a similar fashion, the fabled, magical powers of the diamonds 'Darya-i-Noor' (186 carat), 'Koh-i-Noor' (108.93 carat), 'Shah of Persia' (99.52 carat) and 'Taj-e-Mah' (146 carat) could not prevent the Persian Prince Nadir Shah from sacking Delhi in 1739 and plundering the famous peacock throne and the legendary treasure of the Mogul emperors. Nevertheless, the memory of ancient India as the home of precious stones and jewels lives on to this day.

In the Magic Garden of Precious Stones

The kingdom of the Sumerians and the Akkadians

"Gilgamesh strove to see the precious gem trees:
The carnelian, it bears its fruit,
A grape hangs there, polished for display.
The lapis lazuli possesses its leaves,
and also bears fruit, a pleasure to behold."

Gilgamesh, based on a Sumerian epic, *c.* 2000 BC

Lapis lazuli and carnelian decorate the magic garden of the divine cup-bearer goddess Siduri. Gems are of enormous importance in the Gilgamesh epic, the heroic song about the legendary Sumerian King Gilgamesh from Uruk. In this epic an Akkadian poet (*c.* 2000 BC) described Gilgamesh's search for eternal life, which the gods had withheld from him. The poet follows a century-old tradition and reports that the epic was once written on lapis lazuli tablets. The Gilgamesh epic demonstrates how highly the Sumerians valued this mineral. Venus-goddess Ishtar, for example, the chief deity of the city of Uruk, courted King Gilgamesh's favour by presenting him with a chariot which she had covered with gold, moonstones and lapis lazuli. Gilgamesh also chose the brilliant blue mineral as the only stone worthy of decorating the grave of his true and beloved friend Engidu. The legendary king ordered the smith, gem polisher, copper-molder, goldsmith, and engraver to "create a likeness of my friend … He then created a likeness: of lapis lazuli should be your breast, of gold your body." Engidu lost his life because he killed the heavenly bull Urus, a ferocious beast, which Ishtar, seeking revenge because Gilgamesh rejected her advances, had requested the heavenly god Anu to create.

The Akkadian poet also found jasper so valuable that he believed it could be used to lure enemies of the Sumerian King Gilgamesh. He ranked carnelian not far below it and described its use, along with lapis lazuli, to decorate the home of the gods, like that of the cup-bearer Siduri, who sought to end Gilgamesh's search for eternal life by showing him the joy of living. Both gemstones also served as a material from which containers for divine offerings were made. Following the death of his friend Engidu, Gilgamesh offered a carnelian bowl filled with honey and a lapis lazuli container filled with butter to the Sumerian sun god Shamash. In so doing, he followed in the tradition of his mother, Ninsun, who honoured Shamash by serving as his priestess.

While Gilgamesh ruled Uruk, other Sumerian kings, who dominated Mesopotamia around 2700/2600 BC, ruled other fortified cities such as Kish, Mari, Lagash and Ur. The rulers of Ur especially valued lapis lazuli, which they used to embellish the symbols of their reign, their weapons, standards, amulets, jewellery and musical instruments.

The bull with lapis lazuli eyes, beard and horn tips once adorned the soundbox of a lyre. Royal cemetery in Ur, post-2600 BC. University Museum, Philadelphia, Pennsylvania

Ziggurat in the Sumerian royal city of Ur, Iraq. Kings were buried here with grave goods of lapis lazuli.

Like the *Gilgamesh* epic, the Sumerians also recorded tales of battles and warriors, on lapis lazuli panels.
Mosaic made of limestone and lapis lazuli, royal cemetery in Ur, *c.* 2600/2500 BC, British Museum, London

Precious gems lost none of their significance, even after the Akkadians, a Semitic people, became rulers of Mesopotamia under King Sargon I, around 2350 BC. Not only the Akkadian version of the *Gilgamesh* epic but also the Babylonian epic *Ishtar's Journey to Hell* and inscriptions on Assyrian amulet stones bear witness to the continued importance of gems in this ancient culture.

Covered with Lapis Lazuli

The pharaoh Tutankhamun and Egyptian funerary ritual

"Oh look, you are lamented, look, you are exalted, look, you are strong! Your upper body is of lapis lazuli ... Ra shines on your face, dressing it in gold, and Horus has covered it with lapis lazuli. Your eyebrows are the two sisters that have united, and Horus has encrusted them with lapis lazuli ... It is your two eyes that see Mount Bakhu, your eyelashes will be preserved for all time, their eyelids are of genuine lapis lazuli."

Egyptian spell spoken upon elevation to the realm of the dead

These or similar words were heard when the pharaoh Tutankhamun was laid in his grave and the gates of his tomb sealed in 1325 BC – the end of an unhappy life. He was born in Tell al-'Amarna around 1344, probably as the illegitimate son of Akhenaton and his lesser wife Kiya, who died in childbirth. After the deaths of his half-brother Smenkhkare of tuberculosis and of his father, he married his half-sister Ankhesenpaaten in 1334. Thanks to her pure royal blood he became the pharaoh of both Upper and Lower Egypt. Acting on the advice of his vizier Ay, Tutankhamun left Amarna, moved his court to Thebes, and abolished the monotheistic faith in Aten that had been introduced by Akhenaton. How much he identified with the older Egyptian religion and its creator god Amun is reflected in his wife's change of name to Ankhesenamun. A stele in Karnak depicts him offering a sacrifice to Amun. One inscription reads: "All donations to the temple of Amun were doubled, tripled and quadrupled with silver, gold, lapis lazuli, turquoise and all kinds of rare precious stones." It reveals how highly Tutankhamun valued precious stones.

His restoration policy had the support of Ay, in the position of vizier, Horemheb as Commander-in-Chief of the army, and Hui as the Vice-King of Nubia. Suddenly it was all over. Tutankhamun lay unconscious on his couch. When he awoke he complained of an excruciating head-ache. The increasing pressure of a haematoma on his brain took two months to kill him. Tutankhamun died aged just nineteen as a result of being struck on the back of the head.

Terrified, his widow Ankhesenamun turned to the enemy king of the Hittites and asked for the hand of one of his sons in marriage so as not to have to marry Ay, the vizier. However, after the murder of the Hittite Prince Zannanza, she had no alternative but to marry him. The leading agent behind the assassinations was Ay, who usurped Tutankhamun's throne and later overcame Ankhesenamun, too. In order to divert attention from the atrocities he had committed, he had Tutankhamun embalmed in the traditional manner and buried in the Valley of the Kings according to the rites of the ancient

Gold mask of Pharaoh Tutankhamun, decorated with lapis lazuli, carnelian, turquoise and onyx.
c. 1325 BC, Egyptian Museum, Cairo

Rear view of Tutankhamun's gold mask, decorated with gold and lapis lazuli.
c. 1325 BC, Egyptian Museum, Cairo

In 1922, workers employed by the English archaeologist Howard Carter in the Valley of Kings came across the tomb of the tragically short-lived pharaoh Tutankhamun.

showed that the power of the goddess Maat was developed within him. Turquoise also characterised the god Osiris and his realm of the dead: "You are the one who has limbs of gold, a head of lapis lazuli and a turquoise crown." "Oh, ye gods, ye primeval ones, cross the turquoise waters and come here, that we may worship and save the Great One of the shrine ..." Tutankhamun's carnelians, on the other hand, represented his relationship to the god Sobek: "Sobek, the lord of Bakhu, resides east of that mountain and his temple is made of carnelian." Finally, the red jaspers on Tutankhamun's pectorals promised protection and vital power through the goddess Isis: "Your magic power is yours, Isis. The amulet is this Great One's protection and safeguards him from anyone who commits a crime against him ... This invocation should be recited over Isis blood of red jasper ..." Not all precious stones customary in Egyptian burial rites were used by Pharaoh Ay, as he then became, for the entombment of Tutankhamun. The invocation to the goddess Maat had already been ensured with the turquoise, thus making the emerald and the rock crystal that decorate her lips superfluous.

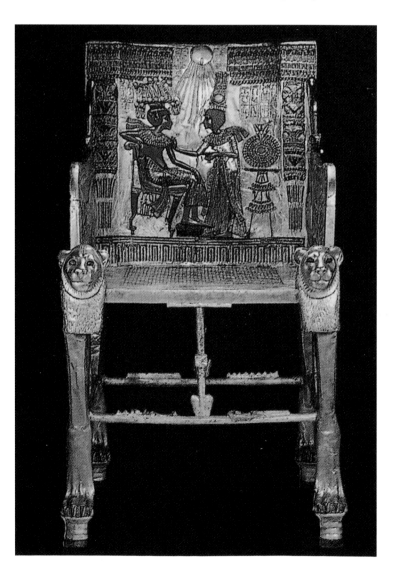

polytheist religion, with his head covered with a golden mummy mask. He was to enter the kingdom of the gods bearing the crook and the flail of the Osiris King. The Upper Egyptian vulture's head in obsidian and the Lower Egyptian *uraeus* (sacred cobra) in lapis lazuli, turquoise and carnelian, images of the regional goddesses Nekhbet and Uto, respectively, indicate his worldly and divine kingship.

The symbolism of the gems used in Tutankhamun's tomb follows the ancient tradition of Egyptian burial customs. The lapis lazuli refers to Ra, the sun god who crosses the sky in a boat and takes the dead pharaoh with him as his son to a new life. Furthermore, Horus appears with lapis lazuli eyes and covers the late king's face and eyes with this mineral. Thus he, too, escorts the king to the newly risen sun and a new life in heaven. The story of Sinuhe, an Egyptian vassal, provides one of the earliest accounts of the use of lapis lazuli, namely at the funeral of Pharaoh Amenemhat I (1991–1971/62 BC): "Then you are paid the last honours, the coffin is gilt, its head ornamented with lapis lazuli."

In order to take on the form of a god and illuminate the darkness, the dead pharaoh needed the help of the goddess Maat, who stood for truth and world order. "Maat is in my body; turquoise and faïence are her monthly festivals." The turquoise on Tutankhamun's death mask

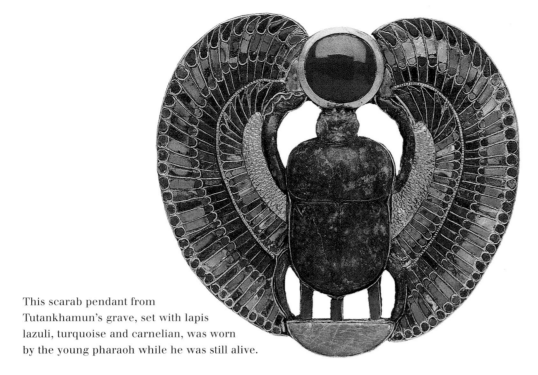

This scarab pendant from Tutankhamun's grave, set with lapis lazuli, turquoise and carnelian, was worn by the young pharaoh while he was still alive.

Ay also dispensed with the green jasper and hence the help of Shu, the god of the air, whose place the dead king takes – as did Pharaoh Mykerinos (about 2485–57 BC) – in order to take charge of the four winds of the heavens: "I was not spit out, yet I became a lion; Shu's power is mine; green jasper am I." Nor could malachite be found on Tutankhamun's death mask. According to the *Book of the Dead* on the papyrus of Ani (about 1400 BC), it was related to the creator god: "Hail thou who art magnificent, Atum, Harakhte! When you appear on the horizon … you shine on both lands with malachite splendour."

Not only ancient Egyptian gods were compared to precious stones and had their praises sung in those terms. According to Ipuwer's admonitions (after 1900 BC), Egyptian women such as Ankhesenamun also wore gems as jewellery: "The provinces lie in ruins and foreign barbarians have come to Egypt … Verily, gold and lapis lazuli, silver and turquoise, carnelian, amethyst and other precious stones have been draped around the necks of female slaves, but noble ladies wander aimlessly through the countryside." Gems also served to represent the beauty of the beloved, as in the text on the Shabaka Stone: "Your beauty is like the beauty of Ashtoreth, your hair shimmers like azurite, your eyelid like an onyx bowl girt with rubies."

Minerals such as halite, ochre, alabaster, hematite, turquoise and lapis lazuli also played a role in the medicines used by Tutankhamun's doctors. Nevertheless, they were incapable of saving his life.

Tutankhamun and Ay obtained their precious stones mainly from Nubia and Lower and Upper Egypt. The costly lapis lazuli, however, had to be imported by both pharaohs from what is today Afghanistan, the only source of the gem in the ancient world.

Lid of Canopic funerary vase made of calcite alabaster, found in Tutankhamun's tomb. The figurative quartet are tutelary goddesses.
c. 1525 BC,
Egyptian Museum, Cairo

The throne of the youthful god-king Tutankhamun, inlaid with lapis lazuli, carnelian and turquoise.
c. 1525 BC,
Egyptian Museum, Cairo

"And the Stones shall be with the Names of the Twelve Children of Israel"

Gem symbolism in the Old Testament

"And thou shalt make the breastplate of judgment with cunning work … And thou shalt set in it settings of stones, even four rows of stones: the first row shall be a sardius, a topaz, and a carbuncle … And the second row shall be an emerald, a sapphire and a diamond. And the third row a ligure, an agate and an amethyst. And the fourth row a beryl, and an onyx and a jasper … And the stones shall be with the names of the children of Israel, twelve, … according to the twelve tribes."

Exodus 28, *c.* 1250 BC

So ran God's command to Moses. For his brother Aaron, whom Yahwe had designated as his high priest, he was to commission a breastplate made of linen and studded with gems as an emblem of office. The description of this piece dates from the time of the Jewish exodus from Egypt. Moses had no doubt seen the splendid pectoral plates worn by the kings, the princesses, priests and dignitaries of the pharaonic empire. The pharaohs had used such breastplates as emblems of office ever since Sesostris III's day (1878–42 BC). In the stone quarries, among medical men and in the palace of Ramses II (*c.* 1279–12 BC), Moses had moreover also become familiar with a wide range of minerals mined in Nubia and Upper and Lower Egypt or imported from Cyprus and Mesopotamia. The craftsman finally chosen

to carry out God's commission for cutting and setting the precious stones for the breastplate was Bezaleel, from the tribe of Judah.

Whereas in Exodus the precious stones symbolised the twelve tribes of Israel and the breastplate was employed to ascertain God's will, during the reigns of the kings of Judah Ahaz (744–729 BC) and Hezekiah (728–697 BC), minerals served as agate and rock crystal seals, and also to describe the splendours of a visionary New Jerusalem. For example, the prophet Isaiah (*c.* 740–701 BC) promised happiness in the new Zion, "I shall build thee a foundation of malachite and walls of lapis lazuli, O Jerusalem. I shall make thy towers of crystal, thy gates of beryl and all walls of precious stones."

Even during the exile in Babylon (586–538 BC), precious stones played an important part in Jewish life. In the Babylonian city of Nippur, the Jewish jeweller Mannudanniyama dealt in emerald rings. And in the Book of Job, minerals serve to glorify wisdom and divine understanding. The prophet Ezekiel (pre–571 BC) also mentions precious stones in his 'lamentation upon the king of Tyrus [Tyre]', who was "perfect in beauty. Thou has been in Eden the garden of God; every precious stone was thy covering, the sardius, topaz and the diamond, the beryl, the onyx, and the jasper, the sapphire, the emerald, and the carbuncle, and gold and yet thou

High priests wearing breastpieces studded with precious stones. Title page of *De vestitu sacerdos Hebraorum* by Johannes Braun, publ. Amsterdam 1698. Bibliothèque Nationale, Paris

Scene from Assyrian king Shalmaneser III's Black Obelisk, showing tribute being delivered by, or from, Jehu king of Israel (845–818 BC). Diorite relief, 2nd half of 9th century BC, British Museum, London

The terror of Judah – soldiers of the Assyrian king Ashurbanipal (668–631 BC). Alabaster relief from the former throne room in Nineveh, *c.* 650 BC, British Museum, London

has sinned, and therefore I will cast thee out as profane." In Daniel's dream there appeared a divine vision with a body 'like the beryl'. This referrence to precious stones as false sacrificial offerings was a sign as to "what shall befall thy people in the latter days" (Daniel 10:6–14). Daniel is supposed to have experienced this vision in Babylon during the reign of the Persian king Cyrus the Great (559–530 BC). Finally, the book of Esther depicts the palace of Ahasuerus (possibly Artaxerxes I, King of Persia from 465–424 BC) in Susa, in whose garden were "pillars of marble" and "a pavement of red, and blue and white and black marble."

The Precious Stones we so Desire

Gems in Greek philosophy and nature study

"Mountains and gems find perfection from transparency and beautiful colours. To them belong the precious stones we so desire: carnelian, jasper, emerald and similar gems. There should be nothing comparable and more beautiful than these."

Plato, *Phaedo, c.* 400 BC

In addition to the stars, animals and plants, Plato (427–347 BC) used precious stones in his dialogue *Phaedo* to illustrate the future paradise where the soul – freed from the body – exists without disfigurement or disease. Above all, the transparency, purity, beautiful colours and perfection of jewels describe one aspect of this spiritual bliss. The death of Socrates (469–399 BC), who appears as a literary figure in his work, inspired Plato to examine the true nature of reality, the values to which man aspires and to explore potential ways of arriving at the truth. Aristotle (384–322 BC), preoccupied with the death of his best friend, concerned himself with the literature of consolation. In his dialogue *Eudemus*, he takes Plato's idea one step further. Although he does not directly refer to precious stones, he propagates the immortality of the soul. But in his writing *Meteorology* he showed considerable interest in gems, especially in their origin. "It is the dry *anathymiase* that creates minerals through its heat and results in various unmeltable kinds of stones." In addition he wrote his own book about gems, about the way they differ in appearance and where they are found, how they are polished or cut and about the power and effect of precious stones. Similarly, Theophrastos (*c.* 370–287 BC), a pupil of Aristotle, informed his readers that like Plato, he especially valued emeralds. "Some of the stones, for example, jasper and lapis lazuli, are unusual in their appearance, but in addition to its beauty, the emerald most certainly possesses magical powers. There are two easily accessible and well-known places where emeralds are found: the copper mines of Cyprus and on the island that lies opposite." According to Theophrastos, there was a method of polishing emeralds designed to optimize their shine. He was referring to 'emery', a mixture of corundum, quartz, magnetite and hematite. Diamond powder mixed with oil, imported from

The Greek philosopher Plato. His later treatise *Phaedo*, deeply imbued with the ideas of his mentor Socrates, makes use of images of flawless jasper, carnelian and emeralds to render notions of spiritual bliss. Copy of a bronze statue, *c.* 348/347 BC, Glyptothek, Munich

India since the time of Alexander the Great (356–323 BC), and the invention of the polishing wheel with a rotating metal spindle, enabled the most famous Greek gem polisher, Pyrogoteles, to polish even such hard gems as sapphires and rubies, which are classified nine on the Mohs scale. The 'Ptolemaic Cameo', in the Museum of Art History in Vienna, demonstrates the degree of precision reached by the gem cutters of ancient Greece.

In his *History of Asia and Europe* (*c.* 130 BC), the Greek historian and geographer Agatharchides of Cnidos writes about the noble residents of Sheba and Gerrha: "The furnishings of their houses were made of silver,

The heads of Ptolemy II and his queen Arsinoe II on this showpiece cameo were fashioned by a Greek stone polisher from multi-layered sardonyx in the 270s BC. Height 11.5 cm. Kunsthistorisches Museum, Vienna

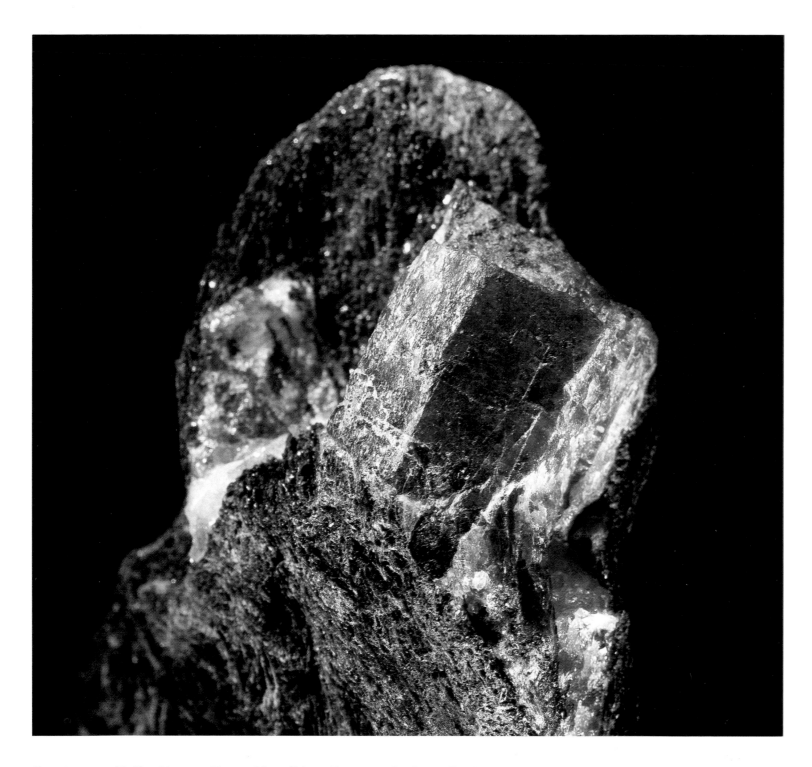

Egyptian emeralds like this emerald crystal from Zabara, Egypt were familiar in Plato's day. 2.5 x 2.5 cm.
TU Munich Collection, exhibited in the Crystal Museum, Riedenburg.

gold, ivory and precious stones." The Greeks concerned themselves with the healing power of gems as well. In his text book on medication (c. 100 AD), the military physician Pedianus Dioscorides from Asia Minor listed one hundred precious stones and classified them according to their medicinal properties. Liquid turquoise was said to clear the pupil of the eye and cure cataracts. A paste made of ground sapphires was believed to be effective against scorpion bites and intestinal ulcers and hematite was said to relieve liver and bladder problems. Amethyst was also not without its uses as described in an old saying which stems from the discoveries of the Ancient Greeks: "Amethyst is the gem, I Bacchus am the drinker. Either it brings me sobriety or it teaches me to drink."

The Concentrated Glory of the World

Gemstones in the Roman Empire

"Here Nature's grandeur is gathered together within the narrowest limits; and in no domain of hers evokes more wonder in the minds of many who set such store by the variety, the colours, the texture and the elegance of gems that they think it a crime to tamper with certain kinds by engraving them as signets, although this is the prime reason for their use; while some they consider to be beyond price and to defy evaluation in terms of human wealth. Hence very many people find that a single gemstone alone is enough to provide them with a supreme and perfect aesthetic experience of the wonders of Nature."

Pliny, *Natural History,* vol. 10, books 36-37

In the case of the emperor Augustus (63 BC–14 AD), more than one gemstone was needed for that supreme and perfect aesthetic experience, however. He most definitely could not be counted among the Roman collectors who took no pleasure from precious stones fashioned artistically. In addition to architecture, sculpture, painting and the minting of coins, he made calculated use of cameos for his political ends. The 'Gemma Augustea', the Gem of Augustus, made around 10 AD for the imperial treasury, is regarded as the most famous example.

In the 'Gemma Augustea', the emperor had himself portrayed as one of the gods. Beside him on a double throne sits the goddess Roma, patroness of Rome. A laurel wreath

Pompeii being overwhelmed by a cataclysmic pyroplastic flow from Vesuvius in 79 AD. Among those buried beneath it was Pliny the Elder.

from Jupiter's sacred tree is held above his head, in the presence of Cronos, the god of time, and the earth-goddess Tellus, seen supporting herself. These figures embody the characteristics needed for world domination for which Augustus alone is predestined. The sun is in Capricorn, the constellation visible at the birth of Augustus. Seen approaching the throne are Tiberius, the emperor's adopted son, who has alighted from a chariot guided by the goddess of victory, and his nephew, Germanicus, wearing a commander's breastplate. Both are identified in the lower section by their zodiac sign – Tiberius by Scorpio on the shield, Germanicus by Gemini raising the *tropæum* beside the Roman soldiers while their subjugated enemies are shown in fetters, pleading for their lives.

The 'Gem of Augustus' did not commemorate a specific military victory or triumphal procession. Instead it was intended to demonstrate that the succession, as settled in 4 AD, was in accordance with divine will. This was of great political import considering that the military situation was highly unstable following Publius Quinctilius Varus's devastating defeat in the Teutoburg Forest (9 AD) and that the victory over the people of Dalmatia paled into insignificance beside it. Only when Tiberius and Germanicus took command of the legions on the Rhine after 10 AD and 13 AD respectively was Rome's Germanic frontier again secured.

Besides its political message, it is the manner in which the 'Gem of Augustus' has been worked that is striking. The two-layered sardonyx has been crafted by a Roman artisan in a masterly fashion: the background is in shades of black, thus accentuating the silky sheen of the figures carved from the white layer of chalcedony. Such craftsmanship lends the 'Gem of Augustus' the highest possible degree of plasticity. Its quality was recognised even in antiquity and by the French king Francis I (1515–47), who held it in his treasury, by the thief who stole it in 1590 and by emperor Rudolf II (1576–1612), who paid the huge sum of 12,000 gold ducats for it.

Pliny describes Arabian sardonyx in a way that suggests he had seen the 'Gem of Augustus' himself. He encapsulated the ancient world's knowledge of minerals and precious stones and quoted numerous sources in

The Gemma Augustea, made post 10 AD of two-layer sardonyx. 23 x 19 cm, 17th century. Gold setting. Kunsthistorisches Museum, Vienna

Book 37 of his *Natural History*. He was interested in famous gems and their owners, in the medicinal and magic powers of gemstones, the locations they were found, and how they could be worked and polished and in how to test their authenticity. Pliny's inquiring mind and enthusiasm for nature knew no bounds and, indeed, cost him his life when lava flows from Mount Vesuvius buried him and his knowledge on 24 August 79 AD.

"Her Shining was Like unto a Stone most Precious"

Early Christian gem symbolism

"And he showed me the great city, holy Jerusalem descending out of heaven from God ... And the foundations of the wall of the city were garnished with all manner of precious stones. The first foundation was jasper, the second, sapphire; the third, a chalcedony; the fourth, an emerald; the fifth, sardonyx; the sixth, sardius; the seventh, chrysolite; the eighth, beryl; and ninth, a topaz; the tenth, a chrysoprasus; the eleventh, a jacinth; the twelfth, an amethyst."

Revelations 21

The ruthless enforcement of the tax on the Jews, bloody gladiatorial contests and unheard-of cruelties, the persecution of Christians and executions and terror were features singled out by contemporary historians Tacitus, Pliny the Younger and Suetonius to describe the reign of terror in the later years of the emperor Domitian (reigned 81–96 AD). It was Domitian's tyranny and the cult of the emperor that led to St John the Divine writing his book of Revelations as an encouragement to Christians to hold fast indomitably to their belief in the victory of Christ, even at the cost of martyrdom in a Roman amphitheatre. The bliss it offers at the end of a godly life is the heavenly Jerusalem. To convey the splendours of the heavenly city, St John portrays it as having the brilliance of flawless minerals: "And her shining was like unto a stone most precious, even a jasper

The Emperor Domitian, who embarked on a reign of terror after the failure of his campaigns against the Dacians and Marcommani in 87. The book of Revelations, with its vision of a jewel-studded Heavenly City, was written in response to the tyranny. Museo Nazionale, Naples

clear as crystal." No less impressive in his revelation is the vision of God: "Behold a seat was put in heaven; and one sat on the seat. And he that sat was to look upon like unto a jasper stone and a sardine-stone: and there was a rainbow round about the seat, in sight like to an emerald." (Revelations 4: 2–3)

A number of later Greek writers wrote commentaries on this consolatory and eschatological literature and the precious stones associated therewith, including two archbishops of Caesarea in Cappadocia, Andreas (563–614) and Arethas (*b.* around 850). They considered the twelve New Testament stones as symbols of the twelve apostles. In the Latin commentaries by the Venerable Bede (*c.* 672/3–735) of Jarrow, Hrabanus Maurus, Archbishop of Mainz, (780–856) and the monk Haimo of Auxerre (*d.* around 855), they are taken to symbolise events in the doctrine of grace, gifts of the Holy Spirit, essential features of eternal life, Christian virtues, saints who exemplified them and people gathering in the heavenly city at the last trump.

Besides the commentaries on the Old and New Testaments, a symbolism of precious stones developed independently of the Bible. In the *Physiologus*, an early Christian work describing animals, real and fabulous, giving each an allegorical interpretation, the attractive force of a magnetic stone on iron corresponds to the

Countless slaves and subjects met cruel deaths in the Colosseum in Rome during the later part of Domitian's reign.

The Heavenly
Jerusalem,
gleaming with
twelve precious
stones.
Cod. Guelf. 1.9
Aug. fol. 68r.
Pre-1350, Herzog
August Bibliothek,
Wolfenbüttel

Creator's infinite love for the world, while agate is the symbol of St John the Baptist as a forerunner of Christ and unyielding diamonds are interpreted as a metaphor for the omnipotence of God: "The diamond is our Lord Jesus Christ. If you have him in your heart, nothing evil will ever happen to you."

Porphyrogennetoi: Born in the Porphyry Hall

Porphyry as a symbol at the late Classical and Byzantine Imperial Court

"This porphyry hall is a room of the palace which is, from floor to ceiling, shaped like a square. The view is of the sea and the harbour, where the stone oxen and lions stand. The floor and the walls are covered with marble, which the former emperors had brought from Rome. This marble is primarily purple in colour, but is sprinkled with tiny dots resembling white sand. I think it is because of this marble that our ancestors named this room purple."

Princess Anna Comnena, 12th century

In the high value she placed on the porphyry of the Imperial Palace in Constantinople, Princess Anna Comnena, the daughter of Emperor Alexios I (1081–1118), follows a long tradition. Over many generations, ruling Byzantine empresses had to give birth in this room and the princesses and princes born there were described as *porphyrogennetoi,* or "in porphyry or purple born." Porphyry served as a license to rule. Together with the colour purple, porphyry was reserved exclusively for the imperial dynasty. Emperor Constantine VII (reigned 913–59) of the Macedonian dynasty

Byzantine emperors from Constantine the Great onwards had themselves interred in sarcophagi of porphyry, like this copy of his daughter Constantina's in the Santa Costanza mausoleum in Rome.

provides an example illustrating just how essential this symbol was for the Byzantine rulers.

As the illegitimate son of Emperor Leo VI, The Orphan (886–912) and the concubine Zoe Karbonopsina, the seven-year-old Constantine had reason to fear for his succession to the throne following the death of both his father and his uncle Alexandros (reigned 912–13). At first, a regency committee under Mystikos the Patriarch Nikolaos I ruled the empire. In 920 the influential Lakapenos Admiral Romanos I proclaimed himself emperor and ruled with his three sons. Constantine VII, who married Romanos' daughter Helene and could prove his birth in the Porphyry Hall, tipped the scales in his own favour in 945 and was able to eliminate his co-emperors. He then proclaimed himself the true ruler and emperor by Divine Right, henceforth known as *Porphyrogennetos.*

As early as the 4th century AD, porphyry, imported from Egypt, had already developed into a symbol of power. Emperor Constantine the Great (reigned 324–37) had Caesars Galerius, Constantius I Chlorus as well as Augustus Diocletian and Maximian, who ruled as tetrarchs, chiseled in porphyry and erected their statues at Philadelphion, or the place of friendship in Constantinople, his new capital. He also had porphyry columns placed in the south entrance of the imperial Constantine Basilica in Rome. Around 360 he ordered porphyry columns for Hagia Sophia in Constantinople. Emperor Justinian I followed his example when he had the Hagia Sophia rebuilt in 537, after its destruction in an uprising. Full of enthusiasm Justinian's biographer, Procopius, described the columns made of porphyry, *gallo antico,* jasper and granite: "It is as if one finds oneself in a garden full of magnificent flowers, delighted by the purple of one, the green of the other, the glowing red and the blinding white of others … Such a work is not a product of man's power and genius alone, but grew out of divine grace."

Some were not so enthusiastic about porphyry and the colour purple. The Church Father Hieronymus (347–*c.* 420) disapproved of luxury such as the gospel and psalms written on purple parchment with gold and silver illumination. In his opinion, such splendour distracted from the holy word because it served the greed of the eye.

4th-century porphyry group of tetrarchs Diocletian and Maximian, Constantius I (Chlorus) and Galerius, made for Constantine the Great, Constantius's son. Looted from Constantinople by the Venetians during the Fourth Crusade in 1204, it is now in St Mark's Square, Venice.

The Garnet Receives its Fiery Lustre

In the realm of the Ostrogoths and Visigoths

"The garnet is a red stone, but a different red than the ruby. When it comes from the mine it is dark and reflects no light. But the gem polisher bestows it light and polishes it, so the garnet is given its fire and reveals its full beauty."

Aristotle: *De lapidibus*, 322 BC

The gem polishers of the Goths were as well versed as the Greeks when it came to giving garnets their shine and fiery lustre. They especially treasured the brown to black almandite, which they found in Swedish quartz mines and polished on the island of Gotland, until history turned against them.

The term almandite comes from the ancient gem city of Alabanda, where this mineral was first polished. The Roman mineralogist Gaius Plinius Secundus (Pliny the Elder, 23–79 AD), who grouped garnets and rubies under the generic name *carbuncle*, wrote: "The top category are the carbuncles, so called because of their

Bust-length portrait
of the Ostrogothic king
Theodoric on a gold medallion.

similarity to burning coals. They themselves are unaffected by fire and are, therefore, often called 'the unburnable ones'. They are found in Orthosia in Caria but are polished in Alabanda."

Between the first and second century AD, the Goths left their homeland in search of fertile farmland and sailed the river Vistula upstream toward the Black Sea, where they settled. The Crimean Goths settled the peninsula to which they gave their name. The Ostragoths occupied the area to the north of the Black Sea and the Visigoths settled in Moldavia and Transylvania. By the middle of the fourth century, Bishop Wulfila, a follower of the Arian Doctrine, translated the bible into German, giving the Goths the opportunity, from that time onwards, to read the Epistle of St John and become familiar with heavenly Jerusalem, which the Apostle describes as being built of precious gems.

Following close on the heels of the Huns, the Visigoth King Alaric I invaded the western Roman Empire in 409. One year later Rome was forced to capitulate. The western Roman Empire ceased to exist until the end of the fifth century. Visigoth King Alaric II (reigned 484–507) brought the south of Gaul and the Roman province of

Mausoleum of Theodoric the Great in Ravenna,
built *c.* 520 by Syrian craftsmen to house a porphyry sarcophagus.

Hispania under his control. Ostrogoth King Theodoric the Great (*c.* 471–526) ruled over Italy, Dalmatia, Grisons, Noricum and a part of Pannonia.

Theodoric made the former imperial residence of Ravenna his capital, in addition to Verona, Ticinum-Pavia and Rome. In Ravenna he built a splendid palace, an Arian baptistery (*c.* 500) and founded a number of churches, including St Appolinare Nuovo (500–504). Bishop Agnellus of Ravenna wrote: "Within this city King Theodoric founded the church of the holy confessor St Martin, known as the 'Golden Heaven'. The apse and both side walls are decorated with mosaics, … [he] covered the walls with various precious stones and laid the wonderfully incrusted stone floor."

"During his lifetime he built himself a monument made of ashlar block stones, a work of astounding size and sought out a gigantic boulder to lay on top." What Anonymus Valesianus is referring to is, in fact, Theodoric's mausoleum, which the Ostrogoth King had topped with a 300-ton monolith of Istrian limestone around 520. It was to harbour his porphyry sarcophagus. Theodoric considered porphyry the only material noble enough to contain his mortal remains.

The science of polishing almandite was not lost during the reign of Theodoric the Great. Using almandite in combination with carving and *cloisonné* work, Ostrogoth goldsmiths created necklaces, earrings and metal brooches called

Ostrogothic eagle fibula with almandines and lapis lazuli, found near Domagnano, Republic of San Marino. *c.* 500 AD, Germanisches Nationalmuseum, Nuremberg

fibulae shaped like bees or eagles. Among the surviving examples is a jewellery ensemble, created around the year 500, which belonged to an aristocratic lady of the royal Ostrogoth court. The *cloisonné* eagle fibula, made of 22 carat gold worked into an intricate framework and in-filled with almandite, lapis lazuli and ivory, was worn as a breast-pin.

King Theoderic the Great was barely fourteen years in his grave when the Ostrogoth culture began to disintegrate. In 540 the Byzantines created the Exarchy of Ravenna. They ordered the opening of Theodorich's porphyry sarcophagus and the removal of his bones. Byzantine bishops denigrated him as a defender of the Arian heresy. In 552 Theodorich's descendants, the Ostrogoth King Totila and King Teja, were killed in a battle against the Byzantine commander Narses and the Ostrogoths were forced out of Italy.

The Visigoths were also affected by Emperor Justinian's (527–65) attempts to re-establish the former Roman Empire. The Byzantine army occupied coastal areas from Valencia to Málaga. While the Visigoth King Suinthila (621–31) drove the Byzantine forces out of his realm, the Roman Archbishop Isidor of Sevilla (c. 560/70–636) compiled a handbook of contemporary knowledge, containing a chapter on stone and metal. In addition to the usual types of marble, he also showed an interest in gems, which he classified according to their colours (green, red, purple, white and black) and their outward appearance (golden or translucent).

He described the rock crystal as follows: "It is luminous and clear as water. It is reported that it is snow that has, over many years, been hardened by frost and that is why the Greeks gave it its name. ... Rock crystal is

Votive crown in the choir of San Juan Bautista de Baños

found in Asia and on Cyprus, but mostly in the Alps to the North where even in the summer the sun does not shine warmly and that is why it has, from years of continuous and long hardening, this appearance ... When you place it in the shining sun, it heats up so much that it can set dry sponges and leaves on fire. It is also used to manufacture goblets."

The Visigoth Catholic king Reccesvinth (653–72) took Isidor's advice and used rock crystal to make drinking vessels and to conceal the hanging votive crown. Following the example of his predecessor Suinthila, King

San Juan Bautista de Baños near Palencia, 661, the oldest intact church in Spain. The jewel-studded votive crown may have been donated by Visigothic king Reccesvinth.

Reccesvinth donated his crown to the church with the letters spelling 'RECCESVINTHUS REX OFFERET', or 'donated from King Reccesvinth', suspended from it.

Bishop Julian from Toledo remarked on the use of votive crowns, "and it came to happen that that very golden crown which Prince Reccared offered in blessed memory of the body of Saint Felix, was set by Paulus of Septimanien upon his own wicked head."

The Visigoth King Wamba (672–80) returned the gem-encrusted, consecrated crown to the martyred Felix of Gerona. In 711 the Moors defeated the Visigoths under their King Roderic near Jerez de la Frontera. This gave rise to the total collapse of the Visigoth culture.

Consecrational crown from the treasury of Guarrazar (Toledo), adorned with almandines and other garnets, sapphires and rock crystals, plus a crucifix used as a pectoral, donated by the Visigothic king Reccesvinth. 653–72, Museo de Arqueológico Nacional, Madrid

Dedicated to the Basilica of Monza

Jewels at the Court of the Lombard Queen Theodelinda

"The most glorious Queen Theodelinda donates this [Gospel book] as an offering to St John the Baptist in the basilica which she herself founded next to her palace in Monza."

Inscription on the 'Gospels of Queen Theodelinda', 603

er favourite son, Adaloald, was dethroned. The marriage of two of her children, Arioald and Gundeberga, made them guilty of incest. She even had her brother Gundoald murdered. Religiosity and lust for power, splendour and suffering, reverence and death characterised the life of Queen Theodelinda (*c.* 570–625). The daughter of the Bavarian Duke Garibald I, she married the Langobard King Flavius Authari (584–590) in 589, and became Queen Theodelinda in Verona. Precious stones, granulation and mother-of-pearl appliqués decorated her crown.

590 was a fateful year: her husband died a victim of poisoning, her son Arioald was born, and Count Agilulf

The St Gregory crucifix, a present from Pope Gregory the Great on the occasion of the baptism of Lombard prince Adaloald. Pre-1603, cathedral treasury, Monza

of Turin (*d.* 616) became her second husband. After their subjects in Milan proclaimed Agilulf King of the Lombards, he proceeded in 593 to threaten the Eternal City – Rome. Pope Gregory the Great, however, managed to persuade him to keep the peace in return for tribute money. Ten years later at the request of the Pope, Theodelinda introduced religious change in the Lombard Empire, which had since succumbed to the Arian heresy. Theodelinda had Adaloald, her second son, baptised a Roman Catholic and a year later even King Agilulf converted.

"We have taken care to send over a cross containing a splinter of the Holy Cross of our Lord." With these words

Portrait of Theodolinda,
queen of the Lombards, on her gospel book.

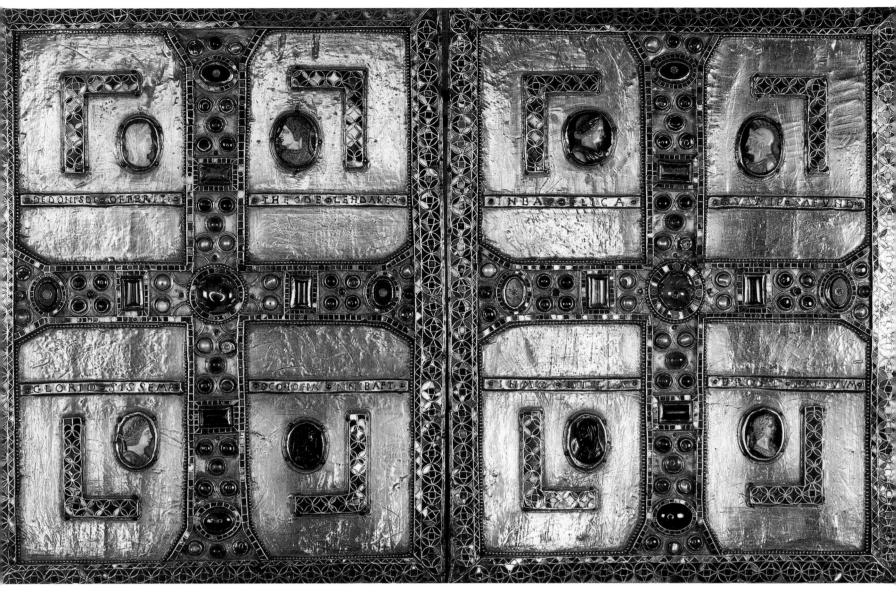

Theodolinda's gospel book, decorated with sapphires, emeralds, amethysts, garnets and lapis lazuli. Pre-603, cathedral treasury, Monza

Pope Gregory the Great despatched the 'Cross of St Gregory' to Monza in 603 to Queen Theodelinda as a means of thanking her for the romanizing of the Lombard court. Gregory had the cross of beaten gold with niello work covered with rock crystal for the relic to show through. He also had a Gospel book sent to Queen Theodelinda which she donated to the church in Monza before she died. The Pope had its cover ornamented with *cloisonné* enamel, gems and many precious stones forming crosses both on the front and back, with sapphires mounted in their centres and set off by pearls. They were not only to increase the material and artistic value of the Gospels but also to serve as symbols of angels, the twelve Apostles and the patriarchs. Besides the topaz and sard, Pope Gregory the Great particularly valued the sapphire,

to which he attributed great symbolic power in his *Moralia*, a mystical commentary on the Book of Job completed in 595.

Queen Theodelinda died on 22 January 625. She was buried in Agilulf's stone sarcophagus in the Basilica of St John in Monza with an ivory comb set in gold filigree and precious stones and with a golden hen and seven chicks to symbolise the provinces of her empire.

The Black Stone from the Garden of Paradise

Minerals in the Arab world

"Pieces of metal that rained down on a cloudless day from a clear sky ... were like poor-quality brass, covered with iron slag like pockmarks and so hot that water poured on them sizzled."

Al-Biruni, mineralogist, 973–1048

The Arab scholar Al-Biruni (973–1048) described meteorites as being like fiery balls. In doing so he was following the example of the astronomer and mathematician Abu Ga'far al-Hazin (*d.* about 961/71). Meteorites are usually pieces of asteroids or of small planets in the belt between Mars and Jupiter, or else pieces of a comet. They come from the outer limits of the solar system and occasionally land on earth. No wonder that the Prophet Mohammed (*c.* 579–632), according to the report by Ibn Abbas, called the meteorite now in the Kaaba in Mecca the "black stone from the garden of paradise" before touching it with his lips.

Legend has it that after his expulsion from Paradise, Adam had wandered around in despair until he came to the valley that was to become the most important pilgrimage site of Islam: Mecca. There a ruby canopy appeared before him as a sign of God's pardon. Under it lay a huge glowing stone whose brilliance lit up the whole valley. What looked like a glittering jewel was a meteorite. Adam is said to have circled this wonderful phenomenon and to have been instructed by Allah to build the Kabah over it.

Bokhara-born Arab physician Ibn Sina (Avicenna) with his pupils. As a doctor, he particularly valued Indian lithotherapy. Illuminated page from Andreas Alpago's revised version of the *Liber canonis Avicennæ*, Venice 1527.

The black stone was to symbolise the human soul shining beneath the throne of God. When the Kaaba was destroyed Abraham and his son Ishmael rebuilt it. This time they are said to have moved the meteorite into one corner, thus indicating where the pilgrims are to begin their ritual walk around the Kaaba while repeating, "Allah is the greatest." Similarly, the seventy pebbles the size of peas that Moslem pilgrims were to gather in the Valley of Muzdalifa and fling at the columns in Muna had a religious significance. 'Pelting Satan' in this way referred to their lifelong battle against evil.

After the days of the Prophet Mohammed, scientific and occult interest in minerals grew. One unidentified Arab author lent his findings on the colours and mineralogical properties and the miraculous and magical powers of stones special authority by signing himself as Aristotle. His work is cited by the 10th and 11th-century Arab scholars Ibn Al-Jazzar, Al-Gafiqui, Costa ben Luca and Constantinus Africanus. The Arab doctors, on the other hand, clearly differentiated between the powers of stone talismans and the medicines made from pulverised stones

Mecca, destination of legions of pilgrims

according to the science of lithotherapy taken over from India. This was true particularly of the famous astronomer, geographer, philosopher and doctor Ibn Sina, known in the West as Avicenna (980–1037), who valued a combination of scholarship, scientific experimentation and political calculation. In his handbook on stones he recommended the hyacinth and lapis lazuli as excellent cardiac remedies. On the subject of the ruby he wrote: "It possesses the peculiar quality of giving pleasure and strength to the heart. As for where it takes effect, the ruby obviously reaches the heart via the blood; the closer it is applied to the location of the illness the more effective it is."

Mecca, from a Persian prayer book, early 18th century. The focal point of the Kaaba is the ancient Black Stone, a meteorite kissed and touched by pilgrims to Mecca. Stone worship was also a feature of pre-Islamic religions in the region. Museum of Islamic Art, Berlin

Sparkling Precious Stones, Shining and Bright

Art at the Carolingian Court

"The sumptuous decoration on chalices probably follows from the contemplation and appreciation of precious stones. The chalices glitter with gold and precious stones ... crowns shine, chandeliers twinkle, roundels flash, dishes of the widest variety and wine strainers sparkle ... The majestic cross gleams everywhere as the most precious treasure of all, shining and bright, suspended from the arches ..."

Bishop Desiderius of Cahors, *d.* 655

Gemstones cast a mystical spell on the art of the Carolingian court. In the abbey church of St Riquier in Centula the precious stones decorating the three main altars, the votive crowns and the thirty reliquaries sparkled in the light of many candles. The sumptuous high altars in the abbey churches of St Gall, Fulda, and St Maurice in the Valais, as well as the altar in the cathedral of Cologne donated by Charlemagne himself made a similar impression. Just how much the founder of the empire in the West was convinced of the spiritual power of minerals, shows in his most important

Charlemagne was buried in the Palatine Chapel in Aachen in 814, along with his talisman and other relics.

ecclesiastical building, the palace chapel in Aachen (Aix-la-Chapelle). He had it decorated with porphyry and granite columns from Rome and Ravenna, marble floors and stone mosaics. Precious stones were even intended to accompany him after death. When he died on 28 January 814 in Aachen he was not buried in Saint-Denis as planned but in the palace chapel. When Emperor Otto III had his grave opened in 1000, relics were found in his sarcophagus. Around his neck hung a talisman, its gold frame and narrow ends covered with pearls, garnets, emeralds, and amethysts. His reliquary bust included two large sapphires enclosing the hair of the Blessed Virgin Mary. For Charlemagne and his contemporaries the sapphire symbolised heaven and their yearning for it and for eternal life. That was the interpretation provided by the monk known as the Venerable Bede (672/3–735), whose writings were read at the Carolingian imperial court. Bede's ideas were based on the Book of Exodus in the Old Testament: "And they saw the God of Israel: and under his feet as it were a work of sapphire stone and as the heaven when clear" (Exod. 24,10). Hrabanus Maurus (780–856), the Abbot of Fulda and Archbishop of Mainz, also cited this biblical source. Similarly, Abbot Alcuin (about 730–804), the head of Charlemagne's palace school, viewed the sapphire as the image of heaven and a reference to the sublimity of the heavenly virtues. Finally, in the commentary on the Revelations by Bishop Haimo of Auxerre (*d.* about 855), the sapphire stood for heaven as the place where the apostles are assembled. Emperor Charlemagne had chosen the patron saint of his palace chapel in Aachen, Mary the Mother of God, as his intercessor. She was to be present during his lifetime through the relic of her hair. Charlemagne's grandson, Charles II the Bald (823–77), learned to appreciate minerals at the palace school in Aachen from his teacher, Abbot Walahfried Strabo of Reichenau (808/9–49). His partiality to gemstones was exhibited not only at his court but also in the abbey church of Saint Denis near Paris. To the burial place of the Frankish kings there he donated the so-called 'Escrain Kalle', a reliquary screen decorated with pearls, sapphires and emeralds. It has often been interpreted as representing an idealised image of the chapel of St Mary in Aachen.

Talisman of Charlemagne, said to have been found round Charlemagne's neck when the tomb was opened by Otto III in 1000.
Sapphire set in gold with jewels and pearls. Pre-814, Musée du Palais du Tau, Rheims

Escrain Kalle, an idealised image of the Palatine Chapel in Aachen, made of pearls, sapphires and emeralds. Water colour by Etienne-Eloi de Labarre, 1794. Cabinet des Estampes, Bibliothèque National, Paris

Antependium of Charles the Bald in the Abbey of St Denis, near Paris. Painting by the Master of St Giles, National Gallery, London

He also donated a gold antependium to the Benedictines of Saint Denis. The *Majestas Domini*, arcades and votive crowns on it were ornamented with numerous precious stones according to his commission. They were meant to refer to the Last Judgement and the splendour of heavenly Jerusalem.

Charles the Bald's preference for sapphires and emeralds also shows in the *Codex Aureus*, a Gospel Book he commissioned in 870 from the monastic scribes Liuthard and Beringar. He had the gold cover of the luxury volume elaborately decorated. Apart from smaller garnets and *cloisonné* enamels, there are emeralds, sapphires and pearls. With the green, blue and white colour scheme that was the sole prerogative of the emperor in Constantinople and his family, Charles was following Byzantine tradition.

Charles the Bald had the stones arranged in strict axial symmetry. While the larger emeralds (eight) mark

the corners and the arms of the Cross, the smaller ones (fifty-two), along with the pearls, surround or set off twenty sapphires. According to the words of Charles's teacher Walahfried Strabo, the rectangular emeralds cut *en cabochon* stand for the four Apostles. They also serve as symbols of the Lamb and the Saviour, who leads the saints to eternal pastures. The oval sapphires cut *en cabochon*, with their blue colour, symbolise heaven as the congregation of the saints. Thus, the emeralds refer to the contents of the Gospels, to the four Apostles and to the chased gold scenes of Christ's miracles also shown on the cover. These include changing water into wine at the marriage of Cana, protecting the woman taken in adultery, and healing the leper and the man blind from birth. Together with the sapphires, the emeralds also made the connection to the Lord of heaven and earth (in the middle of the gold cover) with the saints gathered around Him in heavenly Jerusalem.

The Late Carolingian emperors also surrounded themselves with the mystical charm of gemstones, as did Arnulf of Carinthia (before 850–99). During his constant travels from one imperial court to another and one imperial monastery to another, he also wanted to be able to absorb the magical power of gems while on the road. He therefore commissioned goldsmiths and stone cutters to design a portable altar ('Arnulf's Ciborium') with a porphyry top as the *mensa* and plenty of gemstones. These were to refer to the gold-embossed scenes from the life of Christ (the raising of Lazarus, the calling of St Peter) and the parable of the lilies of the field and birds of the air. Before Arnulf was crowned emperor in 896 he donated the 'Arnulf Ciborium' and his great uncle's *Codex Aureus* to the Benedictine abbey of St Emmeram in Regensburg.

The Arnulf Ciborium, donated by Arnulf, king of Carinthia to the monastery of St Emmeram in Regensburg. *c.* 890, Residenz treasury, Munich

Book cover of the *Codex Aureus*, with emeralds and sapphires. *c.* 870, Bayerische Staatsbibliothek, Munich

With a Sword in His Hand

Precious stones in the service of Asturias and the Reconquista

"Our Lord Jesus Christ distributed all the Apostles, my brothers and me, throughout all the countries of the world, and to me alone He gave Spain, for me to take care of and protect from the enemies of the faith. And so that you do not doubt what I am telling you, you will see me going to battle in the mornings on a white horse, with a white standard and with a big shining sword in my hand."

Alfonso x el Sabio, *Crónica general*, before 1284

According to the chronicle of King Alfonso x of Castile, the Apostle St James the Great addressed the above words in a vision to King Ramiro I of Asturias (reigned 842–50) and subsequently caused the crushing defeat of the Moorish army in the battle of Clavijo (844). The Christian Visigoths had been in an awkward situation ever since the Arab conquest of the Iberian Peninsula. They had had to retreat north of the Cantabrian mountains, where they founded the small kingdom of Asturias. The Reconquista, or re-conquest of Spain, began with the victory of their first king Pelayo (718–37) at Covadonga (718). In this movement the Asturians made St James Matamoros (killer of the Moors) their patron saint and their symbol the Cross of Christ. A later tradition has it that Pelayo and his warriors had carried a wooden cross at the battle of Covadonga and

attributed their success solely to the cross. In commemoration of the victory, King Alfonso III of Asturias (866–910) and his wife, Scemena of Navarre, had this cross ornamented with delicate filigree work, brilliant enamels and many precious stones in the palace workshops of Gauzón. The goldsmiths arranged the sapphires, rubies, rock crystals, carnelians and emeralds in the shape of a reclining number eight, the symbol for eternity, in reference to the eternal life guaranteed by Jesus Christ's sacrificial death on the Cross. The amethyst, to which the other gemstones are subordinated, was also to suggest the beauties of heaven to the warriors for Christ. For as the Venerable Bede (672/3–735), for instance, had written: "The amethyst is purple … and refers to the heavenly kingdom, the human demise and the glorious worship of the saints."

A horrible death on the battlefield – constantly facing the Christian soldiers of the kingdom of Asturias in their war on the Moors – was precisely what was to appear meaningful and be alleviated by the prospect of a heavenly Jerusalem decorated with precious stones. The royal couple, Alfonso III and Scemena, named the cross 'Cruz de la Victoria' in memory of the victories of Covadonga and Clavijo. In 908 they donated it to the cathedral of Oviedo, the city that was the seat of their court.

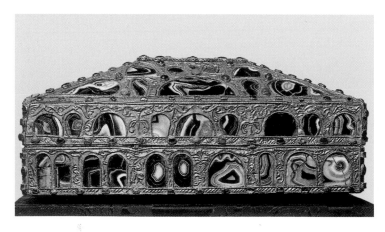

Caja de las Ágatas, a gold reliquary decorated with polished agates and numerous smaller gems, given by the royal couple, Fruela II and Nunilo, to the cathedral of Oviedo in 910. It is kept in a chapel (Cámara Santa) built by Alfonso I to house holy relics.

'Santiago Matamoros', the apostle James the Great, who in crusading times acquired the warlike cognomen of Moorslayer – a useful ally during the Reconquista. Lady altar of San Cosme y San Damián in Poza de la Sal, Spain

Cruz de la Victoria
(Victory Cross),
donated by Alfonso III
and his wife in 908
to Oviedo Cathedral
in memory of his
victories at Cavadonga
and Clavijo.
Cámera Santa,
Oviedo Cathedral

Alfonso's son, King Fruela II (910–25), and his wife, Nunilo, donated a gold reliquary casket to the same cathedral treasury two years later. It is known as the 'Caja de las Ágatas' because of the plates of polished agate decorating its sides and cover along with many smaller precious stones. Like the relics in the box, which were thus protected from the Moors, the apocalyptic animals on the bottom and the minerals themselves referred to the Revelations of St John. How much Asturias needed divine help and the symbolic power of the stones and of the cross of victory became clear when Amiride al-Mansur (d. 1002), the regent of Calif Hisam II, destroyed Barcelona in 985, León in 988 and, in 997, even the Galician city of Santiago de Compostela that houses the relics of the St James the Great.

"You should Gather Samples of Each Kind"

The soul-filled stones of Maori religion

"Sail toward the south in order to discover a new continent … In the event you find mines, minerals or precious stones, you should gather samples of each kind."

Letter from the British Admiralty to Captain James Cook, 1768

What started out as a peaceful voyage of discovery ended with massacre and death. In 1768 the British Admiralty commissioned Captain James Cook (1728–79) to sail to New Zealand aboard the ship 'Endeavour' with a crew of ninety-four men. Although the Dutch seafarer Abel Janszoon Tasman had discovered New Zealand in 1642, Cook, who reached the island in 1769, was the first white man to step on land.

In the process, a native of the warlike Maori died in salvo of gunfire. Ten years later, Captain Cook would suffer a similar fate when Polynesian warriors killed him on Hawaii.

At the time that Cook explored New Zealand, the elaborately tattooed Maori had yet to develop a written language, but according to legend, the seafarer Kupe is said to have sailed from Hawaiki, the archipelego of the Society Islands, around 950 BC to settle New Zealand. The Maoris believed that all souls returned to Hawaiki following death.

Yorkshire-born sea captain James Cook set foot in New Zealand on October 1789, the first white man to do so.

In 1769 James Cook wrote in his log book: "The tools they use to build their canoes, houses, etc. are axes or hatchets – some made of a hard black stone, others of green cretaceous slate. For smaller jobs and carving they use … bits of jasper, which they split off a large chunk." Cook observed the Maoris as they produced blades for their weapons and tools from basalt or nephrite. Since Kupe's arrival nothing had changed in this late stone-age society. The Maoris had still not discovered either copper or iron. They considered nephrite as the most valuable

Portside detail of a Maori war vessel. These vessels were built with nephrite blades and decorated with mother-of-pearl. Waitangi Museum, New Zealand

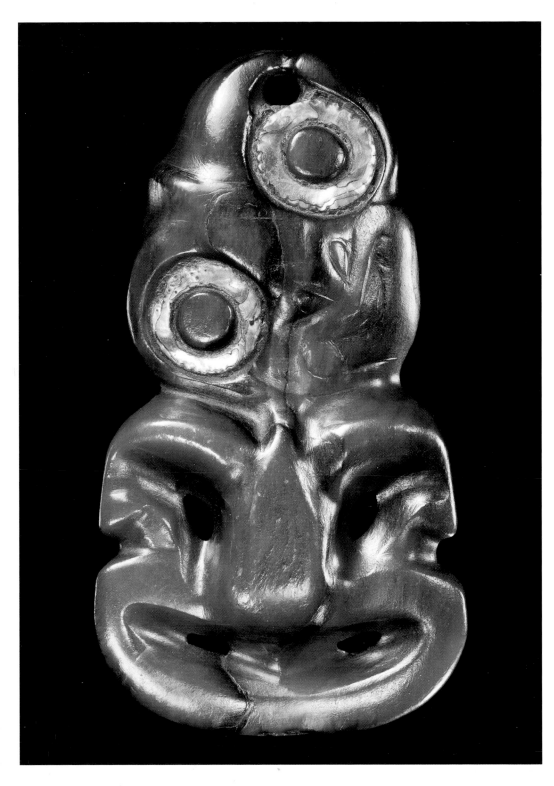

Tiki pendant made of nephrite, being both a symbol of fertility and a breast amulet. Linden Museum, Stuttgart

raw material worked on South Island because it was also the hardest to be found there. They even attributed the stone with a soul that was only released when the stone was broken into many pieces.

The Maori also used nephrite to produce *tikis* or *hei-tikis*, representing Polynesian demigods. The bridegroom placed a nephrite *tiki* around the bride's neck during a Maori marriage ceremony. The *tiki* pendant, at the same time a talisman and an amulet worn on the breast, granted the wearer fertility and protection against danger.

On one *tiki*, which had been passed on from generation to generation, Maori craftsmen carved likenesses of deified ancestors who had returned to Hawaiki and decorated them with red sealing wax and shimmering mother-of-pearl eyes. Captain Cook passed this information on to the admiralty. By 1840 the Maoris had ceased to believe that nephrite possessed a soul. With the Treaty of Waitangi Hone Heke and other Maori warrior chiefs became subjects of the British crown, and Captain William Hobson (1793–1842) became the first Governor of New Zealand.

The Call of the Wild

Rock crystal skulls of the Toltec and Maya

"You've heard about the call of the wild? That's the call of nature ... the call of the crystal skulls ... Sounds are all around us, but the call of the crystal skulls can sound across this sea ... Their song tells of the joy of creation, of the wonder of life ... We can understand the wisdom of the crystal skulls if we open up to this mystery and let the sound come in."

Leon Secatero, Spiritual Leader of the
Native American Cañoncito tribe, New Mexico, USA

Trying to understand the mystery of the rock crystal skulls as described by the Cañoncito Chief Leon Secatero continues to be difficult for European and American scientists. Scepticism and misinterpretation have always accompanied the scholarly debate on the meaning of these skulls. Commissioned by the Maya Committee at the British Museum in London, Anna Mitchell-Hedges from England and her foster father, Frederick Albert, first discovered a rock crystal skull in 1924. It lay hidden in a Maya pyramid in the ruins of Lubaantun, a city in Belize. Fifty years later the five-kilogram find was examined by Jim Pruett in the department of frequency measurements at Hewlett-Packard in Santa Clara, California. He found that the skull had

Based in their capital in Tula, the Toltecs controlled the northern part of the Mexican plateau from the 9th to the 12th century

actually been cut by hand from a single piece of rock crystal. Even today its bipolarity is such that it bundles incident light in the eye sockets.

Other examples besides the Mitchell-Hedges rock crystal skull appeared. Their origins, however, could not be specified. A team of experts from the British Museum carried out intricate studies on six of them, aimed at identifying the skulls' geological origins and cutting techniques in comparison to a crystal goblet from Monte Albán in the Mexican highlands which is more than one thousand years old. It was presumed that traces of mechanical polishing would reveal forgeries. The method produced no usable results. In the meantime, rotating cutting tools have been dated to the pre-Columbian period. Starting in 1986, forensic studies have also been carried out in New York and Manchester. They proved that the Mitchell-Hedges crystal skull was an extremely detailed reproduction of the head of a dead Middle American native woman with a hooked nose, high cheek-bones and thick lips. These findings directed the focus of research on the pre-Columbian civilisations in Mexico, Guatemala and Belize, where the Mitchell-Hedges family had found the crystal.

The Aztecs considered the Toltecs as the main carriers of civilisation to Middle America. Their obsidian cutters, who obtained the raw material mainly from the mines

Morning star temple in Tula, with piers in the shape of Toltec eagle warriors.

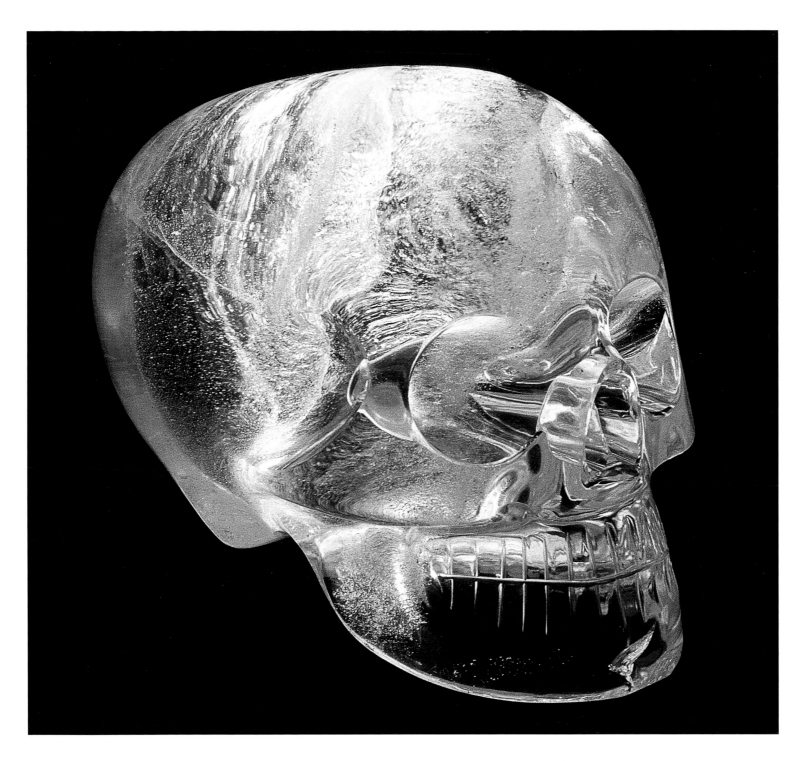

The rock crystal skull in the British Museum in London has been extensively analysed. Its origin and meaning continues to baffle researches.

of Pachuca, were more than famous all over the country. The Toltecs ruled the north of the Mexican highland basin from their capital city of Tula from the 9th to the 12th century. Every fifty-two years they awaited the end of the world, or the 'beginning of the new fire', at the temple of the morning star in Tula. Serpents with human skulls were carved on a wall referring to this sanctuary. Did the Toltecs use rock crystal skulls for this ceremony?

The answer requires more evidence. Some turned up in Chichén Itzá, a Maya city occupied by the Toltecs on the Yucatán Peninsula in Mexico. There, a low relief depicts two teams on the edge of a court with a ball – and on it is the skull of Junaipu. The sculptors based the scene on the ritual ball games that took place on the nearby court, re-enacting the quarrel between the great heroic twins. The Book of Counsel, *Popol Vuh*, the sacred history of the Quiché Maya tribe, records this myth and even mentions the skull that symbolised death and forbidden knowledge, reincarnation and regeneration. Crystal skulls probably had the same symbolic meaning. In this connection there is a platform in Chichén Itzá decorated all around with rows of skulls carved into the stone. It served as a repository for the severed heads of the sacrificed players.

With its 364 steps and its temple at the peak, the Castillo pyramid in Chichén Itzá referred to the Maya calendar. As in the temple of the morning star in Tula, the 'beginning of the new fire' was celebrated here, too. The crystal skulls with their glowing eyes, sparked by the light of a fire, marked the beginning of this feast.

The crystal skulls also referred to the 'lord of death', who was represented by a skull and stood for the number ten. He and twelve other gods of the upper world corresponded to the thirteen months of the Maya year. The crystal skulls were thus part of both the numerical system and the calendar. Moreover, the image of a skull with a removable lower jaw, such as the Mitchell-Hedges rock crystal skull, was used in the transition from the middle world, that is, this life, to the upper world of the gods, spirits and ancestors, in other words, a higher level of consciousness. The latter allowed a simultaneous review of the past and a vision of the future, including prophecies of the end of the world.

The wisdom of the crystal skulls has not been lost. This is confirmed by the descendants of the Itzá, the Maya on the Yucatán Peninsula. Their priest, shaman and 'guardian of the days', Hunbatz Men, asserts: "Itzá prophecy says that the crystal skulls will return, both they and the wisdom of the Itzá, for it is cosmic knowledge … And the Maya will show the skulls very soon … for they

Even today, crystal skulls are used by various tribes during sun-worshipping ceremonies.

are back in their original location. They must return to their place inside the top of the pyramid … Itzamna, he gave us the knowledge of how to understand the skulls. He showed us how to work with the skulls in the sacred sites such as Tulum and Chichén Itzá and other places where the Maya lived … The crystal skulls will … give light and wisdom back to the people."

Assured of the power of the crystal skulls, the descendants of the Itzá still gather today under the high priest of their council of elders, Job Keme. In the Maya city of Tikal, in Guatemala, he proclaims: "There is great knowledge in the skulls and much wisdom to help us in time to come."

Castillo pyramid in Chichén Itzá – here the crystal skulls indicated the start of the 'beginning of the new fire' festival.

Mosaic mask from jadeite and diopside, c. 600 AD, discovered in the Maya city of Tikal in Guatemala. Museo Nacional de Arqueología y Etnología, Guatemala City. Besides rock crystal and obsidian, the Mayas mainly used their 'green gold' jade, even to decorate their teeth.

Saint Faith, Come to My Aid

Pious theft and faith in gems

" 'Saint Faith, a part of whose body rests in this image, come to my aid on Judgement Day!' And I, grinning, took a sidelong glance at my student Bernerius, for I certainly found it inept and senseless that so many people blessed with reason should appeal to a mute and lifeless object."

Bernard d'Angers, teacher and canon, 1007/20

Mute and lifeless is what Canon Bernard d'Angers called the seated figure of St Faith when he visited the abbey church of Ste Foy in Conques-en-Rouergue in the early 11th century. The many pilgrims to St Faith did not share his opinion in the least. They took the exhortation in the *Pilgrim's Guide* seriously: "The Burgundians and Germans taking the route via Le Puy to Santiago de Compostela must visit the tomb of Faith, the holy virgin and martyr. Both healthy and diseased people receive many blessings there." Faith in the healing powers of relics is what drew the pilgrims to the remote mountainous region of the Auvergne in the High Middle Ages. Here they could see the 'Golden Majesty' of St Faith, a reliquary statue commissioned by Stephen II, Bishop of Clermont and abbot of Conques

Santiago-bound pilgrims, in a woodcut by Jost Amman, 1585. Pilgrims following the Via Podensis used to visit the seated reliquary of St Faith (Sainte-Foy) in Conques.

(before 940–84). Incorporating a Late Antique head and encrusted with precious stones, it was made around 980. At first, Bernard d'Angers was critical of the impression made by the statue, her glance, her golden robe and her sparkling jewels. The pilgrims, on the other hand, believed that she was sure to answer their prayers thanks to her penetrating eyes and the magical power of the stones. Besides the Imperial Roman cameos, mainly carnelians, emeralds, rubies, garnets, sapphires and amethysts lent the reliquary its aesthetic and mystical effect. Pilgrims were especially impressed by the four rock crystals crowning the corners of the saint's throne. The encyclopaedic works of Archbishop Hrabanus Maurus (780–856) had familiarised readers with the symbolic meaning of stones. Rock crystals referred to the sacrament of baptism as the foundation for everlasting life, to the power of the angels watching over the pilgrims *en route*, and to the Incarnation of the Lord and the salvation brought by His death. The pilgrims saw the latter meaning best on the back of the throne in the splendid rock crystal intaglio (dated 860/70) showing Christ on the Cross. Even Bernard was to change his mind when he saw the devotion of the people.

The Benedictine abbey of Conques owed its fame as a pilgrimage centre, its wealth, its countless precious stones and minerals in the reliquaries, liturgical vessels and sculptures on the west portal to a pious theft. In the

The Abbey in Conques, an important pilgrim centre on the long-distance pilgrimage route to Santiago de Compostela.

Reliquary of St Faith, first assembled *c.* 980, with many later additions financed from pilgrims' donations. The male head is from a late Roman emperor, the crown is a cutdown royal diadem. The pectoral is Gothic, and the work is studded with numerous precious stones. Treasury of the abbey at Conques-en-Rouergue, Auvergne

9th century, the monastery had been on the verge of ruin. Most of the monks had left for its dependency in Figeac, where they continued their communal life. No one had a reason to visit the remote abbey or make donations. The monks who stayed behind were acutely aware of the lack of famous relics as an attraction. Consequently, around 870, they sent out Brother Ariviscus to join the monastery of Agen. As soon as he had a chance, he was to steal the relics of St Faith – and that is exactly what happened. From that time on the relics of the Late Roman martyr ensured the abbey's spiritual and economic future.

This Stone is the Lodestar of all Princes

The gem symbolism of the imperial crown

"They gleam at each other,
the noble stone and the sweet young man,
a feast for every princely eye.
Those still doubting who embodies the realm
may now see on whose head the topstone stands!
This stone is the lodestar of all princes.

Walther von der Vogelweide, 1198

It was the year 1198. The princes of the Holy Roman Empire were at loggerheads as to whom they should elect emperor. The Lower Rhine nobility around Archbishop Adolphus of Cologne elected and crowned the Guelph candidate Otto of Brunswick in Aachen on 12 July 1198. A rival coronation was held on 11 September in Mainz by Archbishop Aimo of La Tarentaise, who placed the proper imperial crown on the head of the Hohenstaufen imperial scion Philip of Swabia. The contemporary lyric and political poet Walther von der Vogelweide (c. 1170–1229) made no bones about his allegiance in the dispute. His argument was that only a candidate crowned with the proper insignia, namely the great solitaire on the browplate of the imperial crown, could truly be ruler. As an advocate of Philip of Swabia, Walther conveniently chose to ignore the fact that the coronation was carried out in the wrong place (that is not Aachen) and by the wrong bishop (the Savoyard archbishop).

The description of the magnificent *Waise* (orphan) topstone on the browplate by the Dominican Albertus Magnus (1193–1280) is particularly impressive: "It was thereafter seen nowhere else and was thus called *orphanus*. It radiates its light even into the night, and though it may have lost some of its brightness, its unique beauty preserves the dignity of the king." The solitaire was probably a fine opal, which to the Hohenstaufen thinking incorporated all virtues and symbolised Christ himself. In the 14th century, the stone was lost and was replaced by a sapphire.

At the time Walther was writing, the present imperial crown, which alternates pictorial and gem-studded plates arranged in an octagon, was already more than 200 years old. Possibly craftsmen working for the emperor Otto II (reigned 973–83) fashioned it after the West Frankish king Lothar made off with the original royal insignia in 978.

The four pictorial sides refer to kingly virtues: the Solomon plate stands for wisdom and the fear of God, the David plate for justice and the Hezekiah plate for trust in divine grace – the pictorial programme initially related to Otto II and his deceased father Otto I (936–973), who were frequently compared with the biblical kings David and Solomon. The sequence culminates in the Maiestas Domini plate showing the King of Kings – Christ as ruler of the world – with the admonition 'Kings rule through Me'.

The four pictorial plates of the German imperial crown, from left to right: Solomon, David, Isaiah/Hezekiah and Maiestas Domini.

The German imperial crown, made around 980. Weltliche und Geistliche Schatzkammer, Kunsthistorisches Museum, Vienna

The Ottonian emperors were thus reinforcing their claim to rule their earthly realm as representatives of Christ.

As far as precious stone symbolism is concerned, all the pictorial plates are framed alternately by ten convex, unfaceted sapphires and fourteen pearls. In the writings of Hrabanus Maurus, Alcuin of York and Haimo of Auxerre which were read in the imperial monasteries, sapphires symbolised the sublimeness of heavenly virtues, the meeting place of the Apostles and the throne and glory of God. The sapphires thus complemented the pictorial programme of the imperial crown and reinforced the relationship between the earthly office of monarch and the eternal rule of God in the heavenly Jerusalem. Likewise the very number symbolism of the twelve large stones in the browplate and neckplate reminded subjects of the eternal heavenly city and the jewels on the breastplate of the Jewish high priest, on which the names of the twelve tribes of Israel were engraved. Otto II and his successors were thereby making explicit their claim that for them the distinction between the offices of ruler and priest was abolished by divine injunction. The Ottonian emperors also wore a mitre beneath the imperial crown as an emblem of their religious role.

Beside the sapphires and the 'orphan', the brow side of the crown gleamed with pearls, as symbols of the hope of the Kingdom of Heaven, amethysts as ornaments of the heavenly kingdom, emeralds as a mark of the Elect, who hold fast to their faith, and small rubies as the epitome of divine commands. The stone symbolism of the neckplate adds nothing to that of the browplate, as the hyacinth was only added much later.

In the temple-plates, the Ottonian craftsmen similarly confined themselves to pearls, sapphires, amethysts and small rubies, which they arranged around emeralds. As the number twelve already established the link with the heavenly Jerusalem, the lost stones on the pendants hanging down at the sides and the original yoke must also have been sapphires, amethysts and emeralds. The present yoke was only added by the emperor Conrad II (reigned 1027–39).

It was particularly important to the Ottonian court that the precious stones in the upper part of the crown should be naturally backlit by the mounting being cut away,

Relic book of imperial relics, including the imperial crown. Printed by Peter Vischer, Nuremberg, 1487

while in the lower part they should transmit their magic powers directly to the head of the ruler, which was covered only by the fabric mitre. Early medieval writers believed that sapphires could reduce outbreaks of rage, dispel malicious behaviour and avert others' resentment. The emeralds, on the other hand, were to reinforce far-sightedness and ward off illnesses, while amethysts gave protection against drunkenness.

Otto II and his successors were always on the move, to impose their right of sovereignty and demonstrate it visually with the imperial crown. However, once rival claimants started making an appearance, it became too dangerous to carry the imperial insignia with them, and from the 11th century, therefore, the jewel-studded imperial crown was mostly left in the security of the imperial vaults, as in the imperial castle of Trifels in the Palatinate. Moreover, after Charlemagne was canonised, the imperial insignia acquired the character of holy relics. Like Albrecht Dürer, the populace considered the imperial crown a relic of Charle-magne and, therefore, sacred. The late-medieval *Heiltumsweisungen* (relic books) of Basle, Regensburg, Prague and Nuremberg presented the insignia to a broad public along with other regalia of power.

But by that date, the gem symbolism of the Ottonian concept of rulership had long been forgotten.

Albrecht Dürer, *The Emperor Charlemagne Wearing the Imperial Crown*, c. 1512/13, Germanisches Nationalmuseum, Nuremberg

Mix Well with Water and Egg Yolk

Priceless pigments made of minerals

"When a portrait or likenesses is drafted upon a dry wall, it should be immediately sprinkled with water … And on this damp surface all colours will be applied … under the glaze and green there should be a base made of the colour known as veneda, made of black and calcium carbonate mixed together. Whereupon, the delicate glaze of egg yolk and water, mixed well is applied as soon as it is dry."

Theophilus Presbyter, *Schedula diversarum artium*, c. 1100

When the monk Theophilus Presbyter wrote about the 'glaze', he was actually referring to a compound made up of pulverized dark blue lapis lazuli which was free of calcite and pyrite. During his lifetime and in late medieval times this mineral pigment was extremely expensive. Even Albrecht Dürer complained that he had to pay more for lapis lazuli powder than for gold leaf. Lapis lazuli had to be imported from Afganistan because only there were the artisans capable of freeing the material from its impurities. The crusades had interrupted transport routes and complicated trading, raising the price of the mineral and making the import of aluminum silicate prohibitively expensive.

Pigments derived from minerals have been popular since ancient times. In the Egypt of the pharaohs, malachite powder made of copper carbonate, known as 'hill green' or 'skipper green', was used for painting and cosmetics.

Cinnabar, composed of mercury sulphide, was either found in its natural state or produced in monastery workshops. A Carolingian sample book (*c.* 800 AD) describes the manufacturing process as follows: "Take two parts pure quicksilver, one part active sulphur and mix them in a flask with a narrow neck. Heat this over a low flame without letting smoke develop. Thus one shall obtain cinnabar, which should then be thoroughly washed."

The Roman cleric Heraclius (610–641 AD) commented on the use of yellow arsenic sulphide in his work on colour and the art of the Romans: "Gold pigment does not tolerate green, neither with the *folium* nor with red lead nor with white lead." Theophilus Presbyter even reported that gold pigment was not suitable for mural painting. On the other hand he recommended a violet blue copper carbonate and ochre as a foundation for gold backgrounds. In late medieval times the mineral realgar, a reddy-orange arsenic sulphide, was used. In addition to pigments derived from plants and animals, paint made of minerals was very much part of the palette of contemporary painters.

Around 1120 the fresco painters in the Hirsau Reform Abbey of St George in Prüfening used the mineral pigments ochre, cinnabar and natural ultramarine made of

Monks used mineral-based paints for illuminating manuscripts and books. Miniatures in the Codex Ms., *c.* 1255, Royal Library, Copenhagen

The figure of Ecclesia – as the bride of Christ – painted with mineral-based colours of cinnabar, ochre and azure. Seated on a throne adorned with a wealth of jewels, it is studded with precious stones on the robe and exalted with splendid insignia. Vault of choir of Benedictine abbey of St George, Prüfening, near Regensburg, *c.* 1130

Gold pigment, realgar and malachite as minerals and as ground to powder

pulverised lapis lazuli. They drew contours with light-coloured ochre and used the same mineral pigment as a glaze and surface tint for the flesh coloured areas and robes of the saints depicted. On top of this glazed fresco undercoat they painted *a secco*, using the Italian painting technique for dry surfaces. For this the artisans mixed colour pigments made of minerals with calcium carbonate in order to thicken the paint so that they could brush it onto the dry plaster. They painted Ecclesia as a throned woman holding an apple and a staff in the shape of a cross in the dome of the presbytery and used the mineral pigments ochre and lapis lazuli blue as a background for the figure. Applying an extended range of colours – ochre, cinnabar and lapis lazuli powder – the fresco painters produced the throne, the seat cushions, the tunic and the cape and the crown of the personified church, the bride of Christ. Painted gem stones decorate the border of her robes, her insignia, her throne and the surrounding halo

Azure (left) and azurite (right) as minerals and pulverised. In the jars on the left, lampblack and lead white.

and evoke the heavenly Jerusalem in the Revelation of St John the Divine: "Come hither, I will show thee the bride, the Lamb's wife. And he carried me away in the spirit to a great and high mountain, and showed me that great city, the holy Jerusalem, descending out of heaven from God, having the glory of God: and her light was like unto a stone most precious, even like a jaspar stone, clear as crystal" (21:9–11).

The frescos in Prüfening follow the apocalyptic commentary of the monk Haimo of Auxerre (*d.* 855) and regard the jewels worn by the bride and the gems of the holy city as symbols of the strength of the faith and the constancy of Christian virtues.

Precious gems were not only used for the production of colour pigments for fresco, glass and miniature painting. They also served as aides during the painting or writing process. Theophilus Presbyter wrote about the creation of letters and initials in gold, silver, copper or brass: "It is good to rub the letters with a smooth stone, either an onyx or a bloodstone because that helps them remain constant and retain their shine and colour … If you desire to write with thicker letters, scrape away gold pigment in four parts and amber to one and mix and stir in same quantity as gold, be it available and write therewith. And when the writing has dried, polish it. With this you can write agreeably well on walls or marble."

Precious gems were also combined with painting in order to ennoble and glorify God. In his tract on glass painting Theophilus wrote: "If you wish to use precious stones of another colour in the portraits in windows, on crosses or books or include jewellery decorating the garments on painted glass without using lead settings, for example, with hyacinth or emerald, proceed as follows: choose the place in which you wish to position the stone, take pieces of light blue glass, shape them corresponding to the hyacinths to fit correctly, cut the same out of green glass emeralds and arrange them so that there is always one emerald between two hyacinths. When these are carefully fitted into place and set, so paint thick pigment with a brush around them but in such a manner that no paint flows between the glass surfaces. Fire them with the other pieces in an oven and they will stick to one another and never fall apart."

Medieval windows were stained with natural colours, for which mineral-based pigments were used. To glorify God, windows were decorated with precious stones such as emeralds or hyacinth. The Sainte-Chapelle, in Paris, 1241-48, was built to show off Louis IX's religious treasures, including Christ's Crown of Thorns.

"A Godsend and a Cure"

Hildegard of Bingen's healing science of stones

"But the mountains, in which there are so many and such substantial jewels, shine there like daylight. And jewels thus develop from fire and water; this is why they have fire and water in them; and they also contain many forces and accomplish such effects, that many works may be wrought with them. … They are upon this earth for the glory of God, as a blessing and as physic."

Hildegard of Bingen, *Physica*, 1151-58

Which figure of the High Middle Ages more clearly embodies intense religiousness and enthusiasm for healing through the use of natural remedies than Hildegard of Bingen (1098–1179)? These interests were determined by her background and physical ailments. Hildegard's noble parents, Hildebert of Bingen and his wife, Mechthild, were able to secure a future for their youngest child only by placing her in a convent where she would be far removed from the struggles ensuing between the emperor and the pope.

Hildegard's interest in naturopathy and the healing power of gemstones grew as her illness developed. She wrote: "There were many things I failed to learn on account of the many illnesses that plagued me from infancy to adulthood, illnesses that have weakened my body with the result that my powers have deteriorated."

In 1106 Hildegard's parents placed their daughter in the care of Jutta of Sponheim, who was the prioress of the Benedictine convent at Disibodenberg. It was there that Hildegard studied the Bible, texts by the Church Fathers and scientific treatises. At Disibodenberg she discovered the importance of gemstones in the Old Testament texts of Isaiah, Ezekiel, Job and Exodus as well as in the Revelation of St John. She was also familiar with the Christian symbolism of gemstones through the works of Saints Augustine, Gregory the Great and Isidore of Seville. On Jutta's death, Hildegard became prioress but the decisive event in her life still lay five years ahead. She noted: "It happened in the year 1141 after the incarnation of Jesus Christ, the Son of God. From the open sky, a dazzling light descended in a flash. It suffused my brain and set my heart alight … Commit to paper what you see and hear! The story that I saw I did not see in a dream, or while asleep, or in a state of mental confusion. I did not see it with my eyes or hear it through my ears, nor did I see it in remote places. It came to me while I was awake, with a clear mind and through my inner eyes and ears in open spaces, just as God wanted."

These are the words used by Hildegard to describe her visions that Pope Eugenius III, at the recommendation of Abbot Bernard of Clairvaux, recognised as god-given during the Synod of Trier (1147–48).

Preparing for Christ, the seventh of Hildegard's visions. From the illuminated manuscript *Liber divinorum operum simplicis hominis*, c. 1230. Biblioteca Governativa Statale, Lucca

Detail of previous picture: Hildegard of Bingen writing down her mystic visions.

The ruins of a once magnificent monastery. While at her first convent at Disibodenberg, Hildegard was able to acquire first-hand knowledge of precious stones and minerals.

would shape her writings on medicine and natural history that date from a time of great dispute and debate. Between 1147 and 1151, she and other nuns left the Benedictine convent at Disibodenberg and, with the help of the Margravine of Stade and Archbishop Henry I of Mainz, founded a new convent at Rupertsberg which gained autonomy in 1158. Hildegard was now an abbess corresponding with the senior clergy and best minds of her day. She even criticised Emperor Frederick Barbarossa's hostile policies towards the pope. Hildegard's treatise *Causæ et Curæ*, a work describing human ailments and illnesses, their causes and cures, was probably written between 1151 and 1158.

Hildegard worked simultaneously on her *Physica*, in which, besides the preventive and curative powers of plants and animals, metals and the elements, she describes the curative powers of minerals. She also agreed with the views of the imperial personal physician, Galen of Pergamum (*c.* 130–199) on the healing power of gemstones and demanded that equal value should be given to the four elements making up the world – earth, water, air and fire – and man's four cardinal humours of blood, phlegm, black and yellow bile. The universe, the macrocosm, is thus reflected in man, the microcosm. Both share a uniform order. Both reveal God's guiding and creative hand. Man and the universe, his cardinal humours and the natural elements are inseparably linked. Minerals with their power and healing action are, therefore, integrated into the Christian world order. Hildegard wrote:

Hildegard's vision prompted her to write her theological treatise *Know the Ways of the Lord* (1141–51). In it she conceived the world as a place where man and the universe are inseparably linked with God, a view that

MUS UNI NON FIDIT ANTRO.   A 92
CL. S. RUPERT.

Non habitando tenet semper mus callidus unum Antrum, mox aliud quæritat, atq colit.

Nicht allzeit ein listig Mauß,   Sie suchet ihr ein andre baldt
Ihr wohnung hat in einem Hauß.   und hat in viel höln ihrn auffhalt.

After moving her convent to larger premises at Rupertsberg, near Bingen, Hildegard wrote her study of stones in *Physica*. Copper engraving, Meisners Schatzkästlein, 1628

Hildegard's study of the healing properties of minerals makes much of onyx and sardonyx, respectively a black chalcedony and an onyx with a brown basal layer containing finely distributed manganese and iron oxides. The picture is a macrophoto by Konrad Götz of a Brazilian sardonyx from the collection of Maximilian Glas.

"The devil shuns, hates and scorns gemstones because he recalls that their beauty was visible before he fell from God's grace and also because certain gems are created by fire, the element in which he must endure his punishment."

Hildegard also considered the specific healing power of minerals other than those mentioned in the Revelation of St John. She wrote recipes for other minerals, describing their creation, healing powers and uses. Of onyx she said: "Whoever has a pain in his heart or side should warm onyx in his hands or against his body and should warm wine in a beaker over a fire. Remove the beaker from the heat and hold the onyx above the steaming wine so that sweat from the hands drips into the wine. Drink the potion without delay and the pain will ease."

Hildegard of Bingen was thus not only recommending the meditation of gemstones or the laying on of minerals. In her recipes the charging of energy and the internal use of healing stones are crucially important. A comparison with the authors of antiquity or the *Book of Stones* by her contemporary, Bishop Marbod of Rennes (*c.* 1035–1123), clearly shows that Abbess Hildegard developed a new, gemstone-based healing art whose significance is only beginning to be recognised by modern biophysical, mineralogical and naturopathic research. Is Hildegard's knowledge based on visions, did it come down to her in an oral tradition or is it the result of decades of research? These questions must go unanswered although they nevertheless highlight Hildegard's outstanding personality. Despite ill-health, Hildegard's creativity was undiminished even in old age. She wrote theological books such as *Lebensverdienste* (1158–63) and *Göttliche Werke* (1163), founded a cloister at Eibingen near Rüdesheim (1165) and undertook missionary work. She died in 1179 in her abbey in Rupertsberg.

It Confers Strength against Enemies

The legendary history of the briolette of India

*"Adamant, or diamond, is the hardest precious stone. …
Magicians say that it … confers strength against enemies.
With its power, it protects one from madness, wild beasts
and cruel men … from everything."*

Albertus Magnus, *De mineralibus*, 13th century

A 16th-century portrait of a lady, often identified as Diane de Poitiers. Fontainebleau School, Öffentliche Kunstsammlung, Basle

How Richard the Lionheart (reigned 1189–99) must have longed for the magic powers ascribed by his contemporaries to diamonds when he set off on the greatest adventure of his life in 1190 and took on the unforeseeable dangers of a crusade. Sultan Saladin (1137/38–93) had conquered Jerusalem. The Christian army lay defeated on the battlefields of Palestine. More-over, the emperor Frederick Barbarossa (reigned 1152–90) had drowned wretchedly in the cold waters of the Saleph mountain river in Cilicia, on his way to Jerusalem.

According to legend, Richard is supposed to have taken the Briolette of India, a 90.38 carat diamond, with him on his crusade to the Holy Land. Poets of the day attributed wisdom, strength, bravery and invincibility to diamonds. Richard needed a superfluity of these attributes if he were to return to England unharmed and successful.

It all started well. On 12 July 1191, he and the French king, Philippe Auguste, captured St Jean d'Acre. Within two months, Saladin's troops retired defeated from the battlefield at Arsuf. The way to Jerusalem lay open.

Then things began to go wrong. In December 1191, the crusade came to a halt at Latrun, following which Richard had to retire exhausted to Ascalon and St Jean d'Acre. He also received news that his younger brother John had seized power in England. As the military situation continued at an impasse, the sick king concluded a three-year truce with Saladin. In 1192, Richard left Palestine without having conquered – or even seen – Jerusalem.

The Briolette of India, which according to legend had belonged to his mother, Eleonor of Aquitaine (*c.* 1123–1204), withheld its powers to even more devastating effect on the return journey, since he was captured by Duke Leopold v of Austria (reigned 1177–94), whom he had bitterly offended during the Crusade. Leopold locked him up in Dürnstein Castle in the Wachau (Danube) and handed

A king with no luck. In 1192, Richard the Lionheart was cap-tured and brought before the German emperor Henry VI. Miniature from the Petrus da Ebulo manuscript, *c.* 1200

The stuff of legends – the Briolette of India, a 90.38-carat diamond that was persistently associated with both Richard the Lionheart and Diane de Poitiers. Photograph courtesy of The House of Harry Winston, New York

him over to the emperor Henry VI (reigned 1190–97) as an enemy of the German empire. In February 1194, at the cost of an annual tribute, feudal submission and an immense ransom, Richard was released and returned to England. His tragic life ended five years later following a mortal wound in the shoulder from an enemy missile at the siege of Chaluz in France.

Reports of the legendary talisman that had failed to help Richard on his travels next turned up in the 16th century, where Henry II of France's jewel-loving mistress, Diane de Poitiers (1499/1500–1566), is said to have owned it.

However, the high-quality, triangularly-faceted cut of the Briolette of India indicates a modern origin for the diamond. The legends of Richard the Lionheart and Diane de Poitiers must be viewed just as a reinforcement of the mysterious aura of this jewel, which was acquired in 1950 by the New York jeweller Harry Winston (d. 1978).

"All Your Walls are of Precious Stones"

Abbot Suger of St Denis and the birth of Gothic art

"Our illustrious king himself got down and laid the first stone with his own hands; then we and other abbots and clerics added more stones. Some even put in precious gemstones because of their love and reverence for Jesus Christ and sang: 'All your walls are of precious stones'."

Abbot Suger of Saint Denis, *Libellus de consecratione ecclesiae Sancti Dionysii*, 1144/45

On 14 July 1140, King Louis VII of France and his wife, Eleanor of Aquitaine, laid the cornerstone for the choir of the abbey church of Saint Dionysius near Paris. Like his guests of honour, Abbot Suger of Saint Denis (*c.* 1081–1151) was inspired by the concept of the church as an image of the jewel-encrusted heavenly Jerusalem described by St John the Apostle in the Apocalypse. His sole objective was to realise this idea

The choir of St Denis, near Paris. It once shone with precious stones on shrines, the high altar painting and the splendid robes of the kings buried here. Built 1140/44

in architectural terms. The two-storey ambulatory with radiating chapels was to "present the shrines of the Saints, adorned with gold and precious gems, to the visitors' glances in a more elevated place." The choir was also to serve as a mausoleum for the kings buried there. Suger commented: "For the generosity of such great Fathers, experienced by ourselves and all, demands that we ... should deem it worthy of our effort to cover the most sacred ashes ... with the most precious material we possibly can: with refined gold and a profusion of hyacinth, emeralds and other precious stones." He had an altar built in the centre of the choir and decorated with "such a wealth of gold and most precious gems – unexpected and hardly to be found among kings." Other donations came from "the illustrious King ... emeralds, pellucid and distinguished by markings – Count Thibaut, hyacinth and rubies – peers and princes, precious pearls of diverse colours and properties."

Suger's intention to use light to set off the high altar and the relics, to heighten the brilliance of the gold and to make the sparkle of the precious stones brighter and more pleasing to the eye, called for many windows and for thin and graceful columns to support the vault without blocking the view. Only flying buttresses could provide the necessary transmission of the thrust of the walls to an outer support. The Gothic was born – through the mystical views on light held by the 'father of the fatherland', the abbot and former regent, Suger himself.

In the Gothic conception of the abbey church of Saint Denis precious stones exercised several functions, such as to anticipate the vision of the heavenly Jerusalem and to worship the Creator with precious materials. And as Abbot Suger added: "When ... the loveliness of the many-coloured gems has called me away from external cares ... then it seems to me that I see myself dwelling, as it were, in some strange region of the universe which neither exists entirely in the slime of the earth nor entirely in the purity of Heaven; and that, by the grace of God, I can be transported from this inferior to that higher world in an anagogical manner."

The early 13th-century rose window in the south transept of Chartres.
Medieval church windows glowed with paints derived from precious stones.

"This Stone is called the Grail"

Precious stones in medieval Arthurian epics

"A company of warriors lives there ... that lives off a stone of flawless purity. ... It is called lapsit exillis. The power of the stone causes the phoenix to burn to ashes, but the ashes bring it new life. ... However ill someone is, whether maid or man, from the day he catches sight of this stone, death cannot trouble him. Nor does he age, but his body remains as it was when he caught sight of the stone. ... This stone is also called the Grail."

Wolfram of Eschenbach, *Parsifal*, 1200–10.

Around 1210, the Franconian knight and poet Wolfram of Eschenbach (*c.* 1170–1220) was staying with the lords of Dürn at the castle of Wildenberg in the Odenwald forest. The towering walls, splendid furnishings and magnificent court trappings provided inspiration when he came to describe the Grail castle in his Arthurian epic *Parsifal*. The castle belongs to the ailing King Anfortas; his head is covered by a fur cap with a gleaming ruby, the ruler's insignia at the Grail court. The Arthurian knight Parsifal witnesses the Grail and a stone platter made of a large garnet-hyacinth being placed before the lord of the castle. Wolfram describes the Grail, which is only visible to the baptised, as the *hort* (treasure) of bliss and cornucopia of earthly delights. At the end, Anfortas gives Parsifal a sword with a hilt made from a single ruby. Of course, Parsifal culpably neglects to ask his magnanimous host about his suffering.

The palas, or principal residential part, of Wildenberg castle in Odenwald, now a ruin. While staying here, Wolfram used the setting for his description of the Grail castle.

Wolfram of Eschenbach. Miniature in the Manesse Lieder manuscript, 1300/40. *Codex Palatinus Germanicus 848*, fol. 149 v, University Library, Heidelberg

Later the hermit Trevrizent reveals to him the secret of the Grail and its guardian. He tells him that today, as on every Good Friday, a white dove will come down from heaven and place 'a small white wafer' on the sacred stone. This confers miraculous powers on it that enable it to provide delicious foods and drinks in lavish plenty. The hermit also speaks of an inscription on the stone (*epitafum*) in which the names of the perfect people who have been selected for the redeeming journey to the Grail are foretold. King Anfortas had also been summoned, but was punished for his high-handedness. He now suffers unendurable torments and no longer has any pleasure in his jewel-studded bed. No moonstone, heliotrope or chrysoprase, nor jet, pyrites or beryl can restore his pleasure in life or happiness. However, lithotherapy enables the Grail community to keep their king from death until Parsifal remembers to enquire about Anfortas' suffering on his second visit, thereby redeeming him and himself becoming Grail King.

Although Wolfram of Eschenbach did not give the Grail any particular shape, identifying it with an unidentified precious stone, in his Arthurian romance *Perceval ou Li contes del Graal* (*c.* 1180), his French source, Chrétien de Troyes (*c.* 1135–1190), comes up with a grail resembling like a jewel-studded chalice, such as was used on contemporary liturgy. The variation between a stone

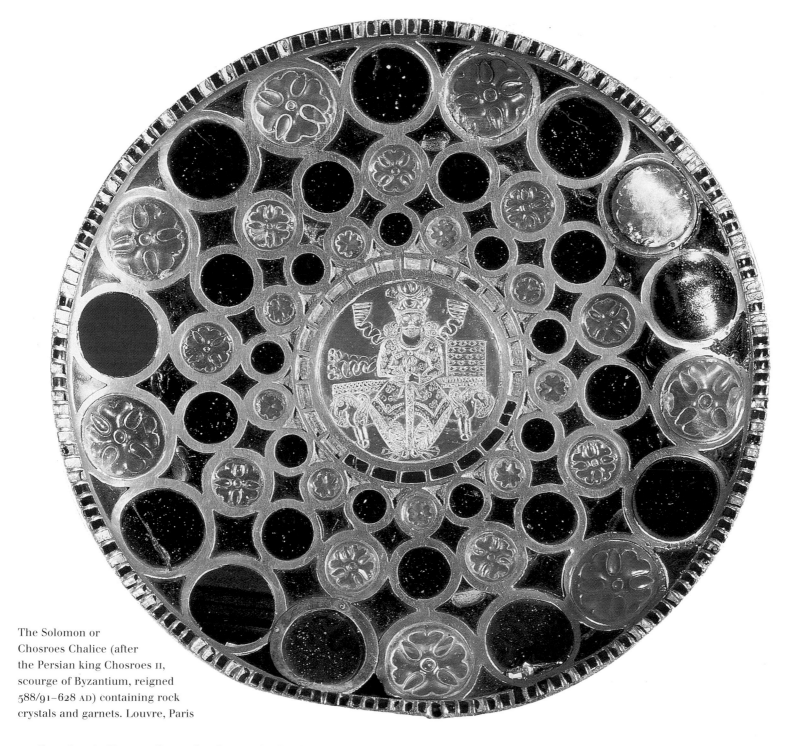

The Solomon or
Chosroes Chalice (after
the Persian king Chosroes II,
scourge of Byzantium, reigned
588/91–628 AD) containing rock
crystals and garnets. Louvre, Paris

grail and a chalice grail may be due to doubt about the meaning of the word for grail in the presumed original North Welsh source of the story. Accordingly, the Grail also serves to store the hosts. However, in Robert de Boron's *Gral* (*c.* 1200), the Grail was like a jewel-studded communion bowl in which Joseph of Arimathea caught the blood of Christ.

Influenced by the French Grail romances, Hohen-staufen poets turned the Grail into a sacred object. In *Aventiure Crône* (early 13th century) by Heinrich von dem Türlin, it appears in the shape of a reliquary made of gold and precious stones. In contrast to this, Albrecht

of Scharfenberg's *Jüngerer Titurel* (The Younger Titurel, *c.* 1270) attempts to combine the Grail visions of Wolfram and Robert de Boron. It conceives of a precious stone bowl that Christ used at the Last Supper. Wolfram's unknown mystic *lapsit exillis* stone is here turned into jasper. The Grail temple was for him an image of the heavenly Jerusalem and treasure house of precious stones symbolising the stars and Christian virtues – Albrecht endowed his temple with a foundation of onyx, a floor of rock crystal, walls with sardonyx, jasper and emerald, windows of beryl and rock crystal and vaults of sapphires and carbuncles. All these courtly romances had one thing in

Rodenegg castle in
South Tyrol, notable for
its Iwein Room.

Iwein Room with frescoes
showing scenes from
Hartmann of Aue's
Arthurian tale *Iwein*.
Rodenegg castle, *c.* 1220/30

common: the precious-stone Grail and the religious
scenes in the Grail castle provided the Arthurian knight
with spiritual guidance.

Other works by Chrétien de Troyes and Hartmann
of Aue (*c.* 1165–1215) give quite a different slant. In *Yvain
or the Knight with the Lion* (1177/80) and *Iwein* (1205),
Arthur's court is a place of harmony and pleasure and
a starting point for knightly quests whenever the calm
orderliness of courtly life is ruffled – as in the story of
Iwein, for example, who feels he is called upon to avenge
a courtier's insult to his cousin Kalogrenant.

Not only does an emerald with rubies gleaming at the
corners play a central role in this conflict, minerals are
also vitally involved in Iwein's quest. The magic powers

of precious stones help him to overcome dangers, as in
the castle of King Askalon, whom Iwein has killed in
a duel and whose soldiers are out after blood. In this
desperate situation, the noblewoman Lunete hands him
a ring with a precious stone and says: "Take this ring,
Lord Iwein. The nature of the stone is as follows: anyone
who holds it in his bare hand cannot be seen or found
by anyone as long as it is in his bare hand. You will be
hidden like the wood beneath the bark." This scene –
especially the magic power of the stone – obviously struck
a particular chord in the South Tyrolean knight Arnold
of Rodank II, since he had the scene of Lunete handing
the ring to Iwein the Arthurian knight painted on the wall
of his castle at Rodenegg in 1220/30.

Arthurian epics reflected the widespread interest of
the nobility in precious minerals. It was not only their
magic powers that interested them. They had notable
physical and medical properties as well. Precious stones
were also used as currency. Jewels adorned armour,
the trappings of steeds, shields and banners. In such
an ideal picture of the world, precious stones sparkled
in every room of the castle, on columns and vaults,
on windows and doorways, on tables and lamps. Above
all, precious stones reflected their owners' importance
and power at courtly banquets and hinted at things
miraculous, legendary and arcane. Such visionary con-
cepts contrasted with the harsh reality of knightly life –
draughty castles, disease and war.

Iwein locked in combat with King Askalon.

Iwein is trapped among enemies. Luckily, lady-in-waiting Lunete, whom Iwein had treated kindly at Arthur's court, appears and gives him a ring, which has the magic power of making him invisible.

Among them there is even Chalcedony

Venice, home of the trade in precious stones

"The floor of San Marco is paved in part with stone, in part with marble slabs and other, not so inexpensive materials, among them there is even chalcedony. A piece the size of half a foot can be seen."

Marc' Antonio Sabellico, *Del sito di Venezia città*, 1502

Marc' Antonio Sabellico could well marvel at the chalcedony, porphyry, serpentine, lapis lazuli, malachite and other precious stones he saw when he visited San Marco in Venice. For nearly 500 years artisans had been working on the mosaic floor of the cathedral: master craftsmen from the Middle East, stone polishers from Ravenna, stone masons from Venice. The floor was meant to serve the faithful, and was designed to be far more than mere decoration. The floor, with its peacock in the left aisle, was intended as a reminder of eternal life and of paradise.

The floor leads symbolically to the Pala d'Oro, the high altar, decorated with 1,300 pearls, 400 garnets, 300 sapphires, 300 emeralds, ninety amethysts, fifteen rubies and other precious stones on the gold and silver panels which glitter mysteriously in the flickering candlelight. Goldsmith Giovanni Paolo Boninsegna created the altar in 1342. The heavenly Jerusalem was to be near at hand at all times, as St John described Paradise in his book of Revelations.

Porphyry, lapis lazuli, malachite and chalcedony were used for the floor (pre-1500) of a chapel housing the Nicopeia Madonna, a sacred icon looted from Constantinople in 1204.

The multi-coloured shimmer of precious gems reveals the Majestas Domini, the Ruler of the World, surrounded by the four Evangelists, the Apostles and angels, by scenes from his childhood and the passion and sacrificial death of Christ.

Doge Ordelafo Falier (1102–18) had the golden panels decorated with *cloisonné* made in Constantinople. He had himself depicted alongside the ruling imperial couple, Alexios I Komnenos (1081–1118) and Irene, thereby hoping to secure a place for himself in the eternal heavenly city. In 1209 Doge Pietro Ziani had six large enameled panels, showing the holy days of the church year and the Archangel Michael, attached to crown the Pala d'Oro. The Venetians had stolen these enameled panels from the Imperial basilica of the Pantocrator in Constantinople. In their eyes the panels symbolized the triumph of Venice over the Byzantine Empire. It was mainly Middle Eastern and Byzantine stone polishers who worked on the churches and palaces of the lagoon state. As their number grew, they raised the native art of stone working to new heights in the 13th century. In 1284 Venetian crystal workers formed a guild. Their technique of drilling stone by using a copper pipe coated with an emery compound or a diamond-studded iron spike was famous at all the courts of Europe. And no city could provide its stone

The nave of San Marco in Venice, begun in 1071.

Floor mosaic with a peacock of lapis lazuli, malachite and other precious stones. Left aisle, San Marco

Venetian women dazzled in their opulent jewellery, fascinating Albrecht Dürer in 1495.

comes from Istria, a hundred miles away. Some of the facades are decorated with blocks of porphyry or serpentine. Venice is the most triumphant city that I have seen in my entire life."

With the discovery of the Cape of Good Hope in 1497/98, the Portuguese seafarer Count Vasco da Gama (1469–1524) completed the sea route to India. The old Venetian merchant routes were no longer interesting because of the high duties the merchants had to pay along the way. At the beginning of the modern era, diamonds and rubies were far cheaper when they reached Europe's markets via Lisbon or later via London. Venetian merchants increasingly lost their advantage in the trade of precious gems. To add to their woes, Florence and Milan soon surpassed the lagoon state in the quality of their polished gems. The situation had so deteriorated by 1638 that an aristocrat named Bembo appointed himself spokesman for the repeated complaints raised against Venice's jewel merchants.

polishers with more advantages in purchasing raw diamonds and other minerals than Venice, with its flourishing trade with India, Indonesia and China. Galleys laden with precious uncut and polished stones sailed into the port of Venice to be further worked or to be sold directly in the many merchants houses that lined the Grand Canal. The ships sailed under the wooden Rialto Bridge, which was raised to let them pass. They brought their wares to the nearby Fondaco dei Tedeschi, where they were sold to merchants from the Holy Roman Empire of the German nation.

At the end of the 15th century, the envoy Phillippe de Commynes wrote, "We sailed down the great thoroughfare known as the Canal Grande. Yes, this is in my experience the most beautiful in the world, superbly laid out and running the length of the city. The houses are very large and tall, made of good stone. The older ones are painted. The others, that have been built within the last one hundred years, all have facades of blinding white marble, which

Bembo suggested measures designed to check the influence of Jews in the gem business. The senate accepted his proposal and passed a law in the same year forbidding Jews to deal in polished gems. The legislation was designed to return the gem business into the hands of those who had traditionally traded in precious stones. In 1671 the Cinque Savi (Wise Five) supported renewed protests from Venetian jewellers against Jewish competition. Only one, the aristocrat Gritti, raised his voice against such measures, arguing that "cutting back on trade is a measure that completely misses its goal. When the competition in the gem trade succumbs in Venice, then the import of other goods from those same countries will cease, and no silk fabrics will be sold because these goods are traded against precious stones." Nevertheless, the senate accepted the opinion of the majority of the Savi and reacted with new measures to curtail the activities of Jewish merchants with the city.

Despite the political and economic decline, Venetians continued to hold precious stones and minerals in high esteem and to use them for the magnificent stone floors that decorated their palaces. Between 1742 and 1745, Domenico and Giacomo Crovato created mosaic floors for the Palazzo Pisani Moretta. They used French marble and lapis lazuli, laid out in designs based on the rules of perspective.

Even the American novelist Henry James (1843–1916) was fascinated by the Venetian stone floor. In his novel *The Wings of the Dove*, he describes a magnificent stone floor inset with mother-of-pearl – the floor of the Palazzo Barbaro on the Canal Grande (*c.* 1750).

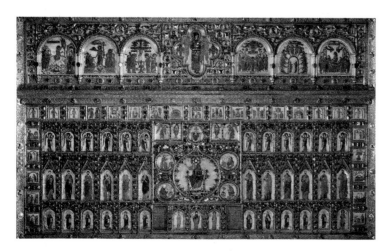

Originally Byzantine, the Pala d'Oro was much reconstructed and embellished over the centuries, notably by Venetian goldsmith Giovanni Paolo Boninsegna in 1342. Various dates from 976–1342

The Byzantine heart of the Pala d'Oro – a Christus Pantocrator panel.

Tainted by Original Sin

Mineralogy and the healing power of stones among the mendicant orders

"Each creation is tainted by Original Sin, especially precious stones which God created, as he did the herbs and many other things for the use of mankind. The power of precious stones is diminished when they are touched and handled by sinful persons … However, the power of precious stones is restored through consecration and holy blessing."

Conrad of Megenberg, *Book of Nature*, 1350

At the time that Conrad of Megenberg (1309–74) taught in Paris and wrote his *Book of Nature* while serving as canon at the cathedral in Regensburg, books about gems had reached the height of their popularity. Lectures on precious stones by Dominican and Franciscan monks were especially popular. The Franciscan monk Bartholomew Anglicus (*d.* around 1250) believed the emerald to be the only gem worthy of gracing kings.

On the other hand, the Dominican monk Vincent de Beauvais (1184/94–1264), who served as the head of

Dominican monks, including Albertus Magnus, Vincent of Beauvais, Thomas of Chantimpré, Master Eckart and Heinrich Seuse, were notable writers about the powers of stones in the 13th and 14th centuries. Hans Holbein the Elder, *Pedigree of the Dominicans*, 1500/01, Städelsches Kunstinstitut, Frankfurt

the royal school of Louis IX of France, was only interested in the use of minerals as building materials. Advancing the knowledge of ancient, early medieval and Arabic writers, he also attributed healing power to precious stones. As a concrete example, he cited the opal, which he described as having a healing effect on eye diseases.

The Dominican monk Albertus Magnus (*c.* 1193–1280), the father of the modern natural sciences of botany and zoology, concerned himself with lithotherapy. In his book of gems he lists nearly 100 minerals and precious stones and gives his readers information about their appearance, where they are found, their characteristics, as well as information about their use and healing powers.

As his sources he cites, above all, Aristotele, Avicenna and Bartholomaeus Anglicus. Subsequently he recommended amethysts against alcoholism, beryl for the treatment of liver disease and rubies in cases of poisoning. His student Thomas de Chantimpré (1201–1263/72) gave up claiming that minerals had healing powers and concentrated his research on their origin, appearance and magical attributes.

Not everyone in the 13th century was enthusiastic about the lithotherapy that the mendicants practised. Especially vocal in his opposition was the German poet The Stricker. He proved that Duke Henry, who had suffered from eye disease and had been treated in Venice with sapphires, was blind by the time of his death. The cleric Volmar condemned The Stricker's presumptuous ascertations as heretical because only clergymen were capable of knowing the true healing power of minerals. Volmar believed in the healing power of stones as professed by Albertus Magnus.

Later Dominicans were also fascinated by the precious nature and mystical aura of gems, in particular Heinrich Seuse (1295–1366) and his teacher, Master Eckhart (*c.* 1260–1327), who compared the holy soul to a golden vessel bearing precious gems. Even in the 16th century, the Catholic mystic Theresa of Avila (1515–82) placed a high value on minerals. She believed they illustrated the beauty of the human soul, a mirror image of God, which she visualized as a fortress made of perfect rock crystals and diamonds.

Lecture on precious stones, in the mineralogical book by the Franciscan monk Bartholomaeus Anglicus, 1390/1400.
Thuringian University and Provincial Library, Jena, Hs. El. f. 80, fol. 245 v

"Your Diadem shall Shine"

Walls of gems and Emperor Charles IV's claim to power

"Your diadem shall shine and your face shall glow since the gaze of the wise, who shall bring much fame through their beseeching, rests upon it: Lord, grant the King longevity."

Charles IV in *Vita ab eo ipso conscripta*, 1350/53

Hardened by great misfortune, Charles IV (1316–78) strove, even as a young king, to be a just ruler and a good Christian. Besides King James I of Aragon and Emperor Maximilian I, Charles IV was the only medieval king to record for posterity his desires and convictions as a monarch in his autobiography, which sheds light on the strong religious beliefs that shaped his approach to art and architecture.

During his reign, work was started on the Chapel of St Wenceslas, the reliquary chapel of the Bohemian patron saint, under the supervision of the master builder of Prague's St Vitius' cathedral. The Chapel of St Wenceslas provided the only access to the cathedral's treasury where Bohemia's crown jewels are still kept to this day and where the imperial crown jewels were housed from 1350–65. Mass was read daily by Cistercian monks from Stams, who were regarded as the spiritual guardians of the crown jewels. The hundreds of gemstones and cameos that decorated Wenceslas' sarcophagus would

German emperor Charles IV and his wife, Anne of Schweidnitz, holding a jewel-studded gold reliquary. Overdoor of St Catherine's Chapel, Karlstein Castle, pre-1565

have reflected the light of the monks' many candles, which burnt continually. Candles also cast their glow upon the altar wall, which is inlaid with amethyst, chrysoprase crucifixes and jasper, chalcedony, carnelian and agate. The chapel's fresco cycle sparkles with depictions taken from Christ's Passion as well as portraits of the emperor and his consort. The iconography, the veneration of relics and belief in the power of gemstones were all intimately connected.

A report by the Faculty of Medicine of the University of Paris in 1348 illustrates the importance of gemstones to medieval society and recommended them as a remedy for the plague. Part of the allure of gemstones had always been their ability to protect against illness and to ward off evil.

St Vitus' Cathedral, on the Hradčin in Prague.

Framed by panels of precious stones,
Charles IV and his wife
kneel besides a Crucifixion scene.
St Wenceslas' Chapel,
St Vitus' Cathedral, Prague, 1356–67

Interior of Holy Cross Chapel, 1365

Karlstein Castle – both
defensive architecture
and monumental reliquary.

St Catherine's Chapel
and altar, pre-1365

Charles IV wanted the power shared by gemstones and relics to be displayed to even greater effect in his imperial palace at Karlstein. Most of his subjects, however, were denied entry and even many of the emperor's noble guests were excluded from it. What they were allowed to see in the Luxembourg Hall was a series of frescos showing an imaginative family tree intended to legitimise their host's authority. The cathedral chapter at Karlstein, however, was allowed to comprehend, metaphorically at least, the protection offered by gemstones and relics. This was achieved through murals by the court painter Nikolaus Wurmser in Karlstein's Church of the Virgin Mary. In an apocalyptic vision, the frescos along the south wall reveal the importance of the relics to Charles IV.

The real and reciprocal power of gemstones and relics was demonstrated after 1365 in the private imperial oratory, the Catherine Chapel. The mystical charm of its agate walls and the relics gathered together here accompanied prayers and the close union of the emperor and his consort – even in their absence – with the Virgin Mary and the Cross.

The Chapel of the Holy Cross was the inner sanctum of Karlstein Castle, of the kingdom of Bohemia, indeed, of all the lands ruled by Charles IV. In it, only Karlstein's dean or archbishops were permitted to celebrate mass. The emperor entered this sacred room only barefoot and

Detail of precious stone panels in the walls of the Holy Cross Chapel, Karlstein castle

humbly approached the coloured beams of light streaming through the windows of topaz and rock crystal. Moreover, countless candles illuminated the heavenly bodies made of Venetian glass set in the ribbed vault and the bejewelled walls. Charles IV had each gemstone section set in gilt plaster into which, for the first time in Europe, heraldic crowns, lilies with lions and eagles were stamped – the emblems of Bohemia and the Holy Roman Empire, along with the emperor's initial 'K'. The Chapel of the Holy Cross unified the power of the gemstones and the relics, the gemstones in the Bohemian crown jewels and the imperial crown jewels. They were housed in the altar niche from 1365 onwards and were regarded as the relics of Charles.

Cut and Polished

Working with gemstones in the Middle Ages

"If you want to cut rock crystal, hammer four wooden pegs into a stool so that the stone can be wedged between them … Take a saw, scatter abrasive grainy sand mixed with water and have two helpers stand there to pull the saw while constantly pouring on sand and water. This should continue until the rock crystal divides into two, which you then rub and polish … Onyx, emeralds, jasper and chalcedony and other precious stones can be cut, trimmed and polished in the same way. You can also make a very fine powder with the broken pieces of rock crystal. Mixed with water, it is poured onto a flat wooden board on which these very stones are cut and polished."

Theophilus Presbyter, *Schedula diversarum artium, c.* 1100

St Agnes is handed a casket with precious stones.
Cover of the 'Royal Gold Cup', *c.* 1380, British Museum, London

The goldsmith Theophilus Presbyter, a monk at Helmarshausen, learned the techniques for working precious stones used in Cologne around 1100. The instructions he wrote in his discourse on the various arts reflected older traditions. As early as the end of the 10th century, the manual on *The Colours and Arts of the Romans*, attributed to the Roman cleric Heraclius, had dealt with how to cut rock crystal. Here, however, the tool recommended, namely the saw, was made of lead. Never-theless, the early and high medieval art of cutting precious stones lagged far behind that of the ancient Greeks or the cameo and intaglio techniques of the Romans. The knowledge of using oil-bound diamond powder (which originated in India) and a cutting wheel with a rotating metal spindle had been lost with the decline of the Western Roman Empire.

Classic stone-cutting with a foot-operated lapidary mill. Lapidarium of Jost Amman, *c.* 1568

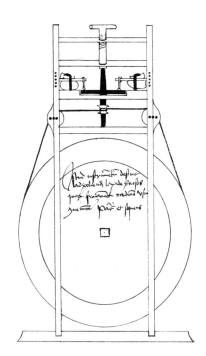

Construction drawing of a lapidary wheel of physician, astrologer and inventor Heinrich Arnold of Zwolle, 1439. Bibliothèque Nationale, Paris, ms. lat. 7295, fol. 137

Interior of a lapidary's shop. Miniature from the lapidarium of Sir John Mandeville, *c.* 1350, Bibliothèque Nationale, Paris

Until the technique of cutting stones in planes was introduced during the reigns of the French kings John II the Good (1360–64), Charles V (1364–80), and Charles VI (1380–1422), jewellers had merely rubbed and polished the surfaces of precious stones *en cabochon*, as described by Heraclius and Theophilus Presbyter. A miniature in John of Mandeville's *Lapidarium* shows gemstone cutters offering their customers rings set with stones cut in the new style. On the so-called 'Royal Gold Cup' that Jean, Duke of Berry commissioned for his nephew King Charles VI, Prince Procopius is shown presenting St Agnes a box containing as many as six gold rings set with emeralds, rubies and diamonds, both *en cabochon* and faceted. This cup may have been made by the German jewellers

Hermann and Jean Boulle, for they were the only ones working in Paris around 1380 who knew how to cut and polish diamonds with diamond powder by taking advantage of the stone's anisotropic properties. A drawing of the polishing machine they used was published in 1439 by the doctor and inventor Heinrich Arnold of the Hanseatic city of Zwolle.

Jewellers first succeeded in obtaining symmetrical facets by cutting crosswise in planes in India in 1530 and, by 1538, this technique was being practised in Europe in the imperial city of Augsburg. The resulting patterns included the 8/8 cross-section, octagonal with sixteen facets and a flat top and the hexagonal rosette known as Antwerp or Holland Rose.

The Spanish and their 'Worthless' Turquoise

Cortés plunders Montezuma's treasure

"We Aztecs admire the blue turquoise, it must be well guarded. The entire treasure must be carefully locked away. If only a single drop thereof is lost, your homes shall be destroyed, your children shall be killed, even those, still protected within the mother's womb."

From the speech by the Aztec emperor Montezuma II
on the occasion of Hernando Cortés' invasion, 1519

Hernando Cortés embarked on an expedition to Mexico to convert the Aztec people to Christianity and when he landed near Veracruz on Good Friday, 22 April 1519, with ten ships and five hundred soldiers, the Aztecs took this to be the promised return of their gods. The Aztec emperor Montezuma II Xocoyotzin (1502–1520) immediately instructed his goldsmiths to set fine emeralds into two bands of gold together with other precious gemstones.

As soon as the jewellery was completed, the Aztec emperor dispatched envoys to the presumed gods, also sending the treasure of the plumed serpent god Quetzalcoatl and fine garments: "The serpent mask, set with turquoise … and a cross mirror of the kind that bobs up and down on dancers' backs during sacred feasts, the

backing covered in a turquoise mosaic with artfully inlaid stones, the spear shield made entirely of turquoise … the obsidian black sandals, … Tlaloc's serpent earring made of green gemstones … and his serpent staff cut from turquoise." The messengers presented this treasure to Hernando Cortés, fastening the turquoise mask to his face and fitting the chain of green gemstones around his neck. But Cortés failed to recognize the honour that was being bestowed upon him, as well as the material and symbolic value of the turquoise. Instead, he was dissatisfied with the gifts, fired shots from his ships and engaged the Tlaxcaltecs as his allies to attack Montezuma's empire. "The Spanish soldiers stood on the side of the roads and searched the fleeing people. All they wanted was gold. Jade, turquoise and quetzal feathers were worthless to them … Only for gold did the Spaniards hunger and thirst, it is true … like hungry pigs they rooted for gold …," as the tale is told in the Aztec *Codex Florentino*.

Despite the Spanish raids, Montezuma received the Spaniards on 8 November, in the capital Tenochtitlán, a city of more than 250,000 inhabitants. Cortés, however, simply had the emperor arrested and raided his treasury. They melted the gold into bars and took only the best of the valuable, green gemstones; the others were

Flat Commander Hernando Cortés. 17th-century painting by Sánchez Coello.

Montezuma II, last Aztec emperor of Mexico on a painting from the 2nd half of the 16th century. Soprintendenza per i Beni Artistici e Storici, Florence

Mask made of wood, turquoise, jadeite and shells – one of the most valuable and best-preserved pieces of its kind. Museo Nazionale Preistorico ed Etnografico 'L Pigorini', Rome

stolen by the Tlaxcaltecs. All of Montezuma's treasures were hauled out, among them the crown of turquoise mosaic with a vertical triangular front piece, the nose guard in turquoise and the emperor's entire wardrobe.

Cortés, who had been charged with introducing the Christian faith, was now ruling over Montezuma's empire. To punish him for his high-handed approach, Diego Velázquez, the governor of Cuba, dispatched eighteen ships to Mexico in 1520 under the command of Pánfilo de Narváez. Cortés immediately left Tenochtitlán, defeated his enemies in battle and reinforced his army with deserting soldiers and captured weapons and artillery.

In the meantime, Pedro de Alvarado tried to defend the Spanish interests in Tenochtitlán. During the feast held in honour of the god Huitzilopochtli, Alvarado noticed the high esteem in which the Aztecs held their turquoise – not only as decoration for their symbols of power but also in celebration of their cult. "The priests began to shape the figure of Huitzilopochtli … and adorned him with his serpent earring fashioned of turquoise mosaic… ." At the height of the feast, the Spaniards, however, suddenly attacked the dancers, stabbed them, ran their swords through them and beat them to death. Despite the bloodbath, Montezuma – imprisoned and cast in chains – made an appeal for prudence. But the Aztec warriors rose in rebellion, killing all royal servants, who were recognizable by a lip stud made of mountain crystal. On the following day, 27 June 1520, Montezuma II died, and the Spaniards tossed his corpse in front of the door of his palace.

The Aztecs elected Montezuma's war-mongering brother Cuitláhuac (1520) as their new emperor, who succeeded in forcing Cortés to retreat from Tenochtitlán. The Aztecs took advantage of their victory to "once again adorn the images, which embodied the gods in the festivities, with necklaces and jewels and to dress them in turquoise masks … ," and Emperor Cuitláhuac joined forces with chancellor Tlacotzin to organize a resistance movement: "Mexicans, the might of Huitzilopochtli lies in these jewels. Throw the sacred spear, the spear with the obsidian tip, at our enemies, for it is the fire serpent, the arrow that pierces fire." As with turquoise, obsidian served the Aztecs as adornment, cult object and war symbol. But emperor Cuitláhuac's days were numbered. The smallpox epidemic, which the Spaniards had spread, claimed his life and he was succeeded by his cousin Cuauhtémoc (1520–25). Even by uniting their forces under his leadership, the Aztecs were unable to repel the Spanish. On 13 August 1521, the supreme commander Cortés, together with Prince Ixtlilxóchitl of Texcoco, stormed the capital. Cuauhtémoc capitulated and was taken prisoner. The Spaniards divided all the gold and silver among themselves on the very same day, but left the feathers and precious stones for the allied Texcoco chiefs.

The Aztec chiefs continued to resist, but five days later they were also defeated and another two thousand warriors had fallen – the battle was over. "Gold, jade, valuable robes, quetzal feathers, all that was once precious, is now worthless … ," remarked an anonymous witness. Mexico was now completely in the hands of the Spanish. The Hapsburg emperor Charles v appointed Cortés as governor of New Spain.

Surrounded by water: Tenochtitlán at the time of the last Aztec rulers. Museo Nacional de Antropología e Historia, Mexico City

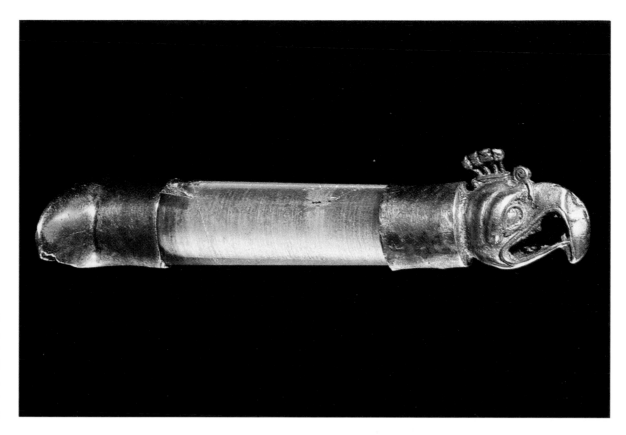

Gold lip-piece
made of rock crystal,
which the Aztec ruler
Montezuma II awarded
his bodyguard.
Museum für
Völkerkunde, Vienna

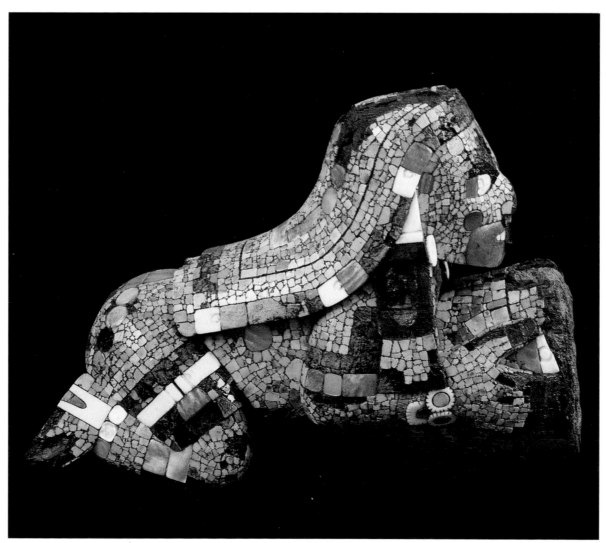

Knife handle made
of wood, turquoise,
jadeite and shell.
Museo Nazionale
Preistorico ed
Etnografico
'L Pigorini', Rome

The Garden of Health

Lithotherapy at the dawn of the Modern Age

"The hematite or bloodstone ... is cold and dry by nature. When the stone is held during a nosebleed, it alleviates bleeding. Pulverized and mixed with the juice of herbs and spread inside the nostrils, this stone stops nosebleeds."

Johann Wonnecke of Cube: *Hortus sanitatis*, 1485

Because water turns red during its polishing, the hematite or bloodstone has always been associated with the human circulatory system. Johann Wonnecke of Cube also subscribed to this belief. As a city physician in Frankfurt am Main (1484–89) he wrote *The Garden of Health*, in which he recommended the use of hematite for the relief of nosebleeds, to stem internal bleeding and to relieve menstrual complaints. In his lithotherapeutic treatment for the removal of bladder stones, he also experimented with the effects of hyacinth, sapphires, rock crystals and other stones known for their healing properties, thereby advancing the highly regarded medieval art of using gems for their medicinal properties. Thanks to the printing techniques mastered by Peter Schloffer, Jakob Meydenbach and Johann Prüß, Cube's discoveries became widely circulated.

Theophrastus Bombastus of Hohenheim, better known as Paracelsus. 16th-century oil painting, Painting Gallery, Nancy

In a satirical poem written around 1250, however, a writer poked fun at the miraculous healing powers of minerals and condemned the sale of precious healing gems as blatant commercialism. The poem maintained that a piece of coloured glass could please the eye as well as an expensive, sparkling precious stone. Similarily, the physician, lawyer and philosopher Henricus Cornelius Agrippa of Nettesheim (1486–1535) also rejected critical comments. During his tenure as professor at the University of Dôle, he wrote his *Secret Philosophy* in 1509. The work is a defense of magic, which allows man to unravel the mysteries of nature, including the relationship of precious stones to the stars, from which minerals derive their healing powers. As a result of his work, Agrippa was persecuted as a heretic and in 1530 imprisoned in the Debtor's Tower in Brussels.

Philippus Aureolus Theophrastus Bombastus of Hohenheim, also known as Paracelsus (1493/4–1541), was a physician and university professor from Basle who took a different approach. His healing treatments were based not on magic and astrology but on figures, empirical evidence, verifiable facts and thorough knowledge of his subject. There was no room in his findings for unidentifiable mixtures or attractive precious gems. Instead, Paracelsus, the founder of scientific medicine, demanded that substances used for healing show concrete and consistent results. Nevertheless, minerals like hematite, sulphur or antimony still played an import role as medication in his medical practice.

Stopping nosebleeds with hematite. Woodcut from *Hortus sanitatis*, 1507

The search for healing stones. Woodcut from *Hortus sanitatis*, c. 1500. Landes- und Hochschulbibliothek, Darmstadt, Sign. Inkunabel III 68, fol. 310r

Hematite (iron oxide),
red iron ore.
Private collection

Among minerals, he differentiated between their 'salt', which characterizes the colour and flocculation, their 'sulphur', which is responsible for structure, substance and their construction and their 'mercury', which lends the stones their power. Commenting on mineral spas, Paracelsus remarked: "There are a number of spas that have the power and the force to expell diseases."

The inhalation of sulphur fumes in spas and the tiniest particles of halite are still accepted today by traditional medicine as healing therapies.

Locked in the Vaults for Ever

Precious stones in the Wittelsbach treasury

"We therefore ordain and decree that our family and domestic jewellery ... should remain for ever here in Munich in the Neuveste, the electoral seat adequate for this purpose."

Decree by Duke Albrecht of Bavaria
and his wife, Anne of Austria, 1565

The treasure vaults constructed under Duke Albrecht v (reigned 1550–79) were located in the Silver Tower, which formed part of the original fortifications of the Neuveste, in Munich. They sparkled with rock crystals, sapphires and other precious stones included in the family jewellery. At the end of his reign, Albrecht's son and successor, Duke William v (reigned 1579–97), added to it the statuette of the knight of St George, to a design by the court architect Friedrich Sustris.

Cut rubies mark the saint's crest (*cimier*) and the plumes of the grey and chestnut steed made of chalcedony. Rubies polished flat and arranged in crosses decorate the white enamelled armour of the horse, while drop-shaped rubies dangle from the saddlecloth. The hapless dragon beneath the horse's feet is dotted with round,

Statue of Duke Albrecht v, founder of the treasury of the House of Wittelsbach and associated art collection. Hans Krumper, 1619/22, Cathedral, Munich

irregularly arranged rubies on its head and belly. The blade of St George's sword and the dragon's teeth are made of rock crystal; the horse's eyes of shimmering opals. The diamonds all over the statue indicate the state of contemporary diamond cutting – their simple facet cut is documented in Augsburg from 1538.

Unlike in the Middle Ages, the minerals on the statuette symbolised neither Christian nor any other virtues. The precious stones were intended to ennoble, to decorate and to convey a degree of realism – the rubies, for example, serve to illustrate the blood of the dragon in its death throes. Neither stone symbolism nor magic play any part. As the twelve books on mining and metallurgy written in the 16th century by the contemporary physician and natural scientist Georgius Agricola (1494–1555) indicate, the foundations were well established for a study of scientific minerals.

Nonetheless, the statuette was not principally about science or even art. The figure of St George and the dragon was used by Duke William v as a receptacle for the highly popular relic of St George. Precious stones were being co-opted as weapons in the Counter Reformation's struggle with Protestantism at that time. The reliquary was likewise particularly valued by the Elector Maximilian I of Bavaria when the conflict between the Catholic League and the Protestant Union reached a climax in the bloody Thirty Years' War. He commissioned Stephan Hoetzer to make a plinth for the statue displaying

Crystal shrine of Duke Albrecht v, made 1560/70 by the Milanese craftsman Annibale Fontana. The ebony casket is by Augsburg casket-makers and goldsmiths. Treasury, Munich Residenz

Statuette of St George,
1586/97 and 1638/41
(pedestal). Treasury,
Munich Residenz

the Bavarian arms (1638–41). The sapphires on the lozenge shield were intended to emphasise the loyalty of the Bavarian Wittelsbachs to the Catholic faith.

The dukes of Bavaria did not only employ local stone cutters for their family treasure. Albrecht v, for example, brought in master rock-crystal cutter Annibale Fontana of Milan (1540–1587) to make the crystal shrine. His fellow countrymen, the Sarachi brothers, were principally engaged on stone pieces for the art collection housed in the former stables in Munich. Following a scheme evolved by the court physician Samuel à Quiccheberg, the doyen of princely art collections, to create an appropriate setting, the idea of a ducal *Wunderkammer* (curiosity cabinet) of the known and empirically verifiable world was realised.

Reflection and Radiance of the Godhead

In the service of the Emperor Rudolph II

"The emperor loves precious stones not as a means of enhancing his own dignity and majesty, whose greatness requires no external support, but to contemplate the greatness and ineffable power of God in the stones, which unite the beauty of the whole world in such tiny bodies."

Anselmus Boetius de Boodt,
Gemmarum et lapidum historia, 1609

Having surrendered military leadership, lost Hungary, Moravia and Austria to his brother Matthias and been deposed as Emperor of the Holy Roman Empire, the Habsburg ruler Rudolph II (1552–1612) capped the succession of disasters at the end of his reign by developing a stomach complaint.

Although his last years were most unfortunate, his court in its heyday, after he had finally moved to Prague in 1583, had been splendid. Focusing on the emperor's days of glory, his personal physician Anselmus Boetius de Boodt describes Rudolph's uncommon interest in polished minerals and crystal, which in his view embodied the "reflection and radiance of the godhead." In 1588 Rudolph issued general instructions for minerals to be sought in all countries subject to the crown of Bohemia, in order to increase the variety and wealth of his art collection in Prague. Prospecting for precious stones became an imperial prerogative.

Cameo with the silhouette of the Emperor Rudolf II, made of polished chalcedony. Ottavio Miseroni, *c.* 1590. Kunsthistorisches Museum, Vienna

In the same year, Rudolph also summoned Milanese stone cutter Ottavio Miseroni (1567–1624) to Prague. The Miseroni workshop had become the leading stone-cutting workshop in Milan under the guidance of Ottavio's father and uncle, Girolamo and Gasparo. Taking their tradition forward, Ottavio established a workshop in Prague whose bowls, plates and jugs made of prase, jasper, rock crystal, smoky quartz, lapis lazuli, nephrite, moss agate, heliotrope and other minerals became all the rage. The oldest documented polished work by Ottavio is a cameo of the emperor from polished chalcedony (*c.* 1590).

Mosaic of the Hradčin in Prague, seat of government of the German emperor Rudolf II from 1583. Made in various stones post-1601 by the workshop of Cosimo and Giovanni Castrucci. Art and Crafts Museum, Prague

Imperial crown of Rudolf II made by Jan Vermeyen, with a sapphire topstone symbolising Heaven. Weltliche und Geistliche Schatzkammer, Vienna

The so-called Bezoar cup by Jan Vermeyen, 1602. Rudolf II normally drank from this to frustrate attempts to poison him. Kunsthistorisches Museum, Vienna

Assisting the Miseronis was the Brussels-born, private imperial goldsmith Jan Vermeyen (pre-1559–1606), who created Rudolph's crown (1602) and the Bezoar cup (1602) for his Prague art collection. Bezoars are stones found in the stomachs of Asiatic bezoar goats or South American llamas, and have been used ever since the days of the Arab physician Ibn Zohr (1091–1161) in powder form as an antidote to all kinds of poison and to treat numerous illnesses. Rudolph himself was quite persuaded of the detoxifying effect of bezoars, and always drank from the Bezoar cup to forestall any furtive attempts to poison him and also to alleviate his melancholy.

The Florentine Castrucci family of artists likewise worked for the emperor as his private stone cutters, making mosaics of hard polished stone in the *pietra dura* technique. Cosimo and Giovanni Castrucci were able to assemble flat stones of jasper, agate, carnelian and other minerals so as to produce ornamental motifs, imperial armorial devices, landscapes and *vedute*, including a prospect of the Hradčin castle (shown on previous page) in Prague (post-1601). According to Anselmus, all this came about just so that Rudolph could contemplate the ineffable power of God in his art cabinet.

The Eighth Wonder of the World

The story of the Amber Room

"The style of the Amber Room of Tsarskoye Selo is a mixture of baroque and rococo, and is a real marvel, not just because of the great value of the materials, the elaborate carving and lightness of forms, but principally because of the glorious colour of the amber, sometimes dark, sometimes light, but always lending the whole room an inexpressible charm."

Baron A. von Fölkersam, 1912

Thirty-thousand-year-old necklaces and charms testify to the long human fascination with amber, the 'Gold of the North'. Its attraction lasted even into the 18th century. When the Elector of Brandenburg, Frederick III (1657–1713), crowned himself King Frederick I of Prussia in Königsberg on 18 January 1701, he, too, came to know a passion for the fossilized resin from the shores of the Baltic. That same year, he commissioned the Danish craftsman Gottfried Wolffram to carve an amber chamber for the royal palace at Charlottenburg. Wolffram fell out of favour in 1707, however, and was replaced by the Danzig craftsmen Ernst Schacht and Gotfried Turow, who completed the amber panels by 1711. They were not, as planned, used to grace Charlottenburg Palace but were instead installed in the smoking room of the royal palace in Berlin, where the Russian tsar, Peter I, saw the Amber Room in 1716. He had gone to Berlin to forge an alliance with Frederick's son and successor, Frederick William I (1688–1740), against Charles XII of Sweden. In view of the occasion, the Prussian king gifted the Amber Room to the tsar. The editors of the *Correspondenz* newspaper, Zacharias Grübel and Franz Herrmann Ortgies, commented at the time: "The degree of understanding between the two rulers may also be judged by the king's presentation to the tsar of two sumptuous gifts: a magnificent and exquisite ship and enough precious amber panelling, itself worth almost thirty thousand imperial thalers, to line a chamber." The Amber Room, packed into eighteen crates, was taken by horse and cart to St Petersburg in April 1717.

The crates were at first stored until 1723–24 in the old Winter House before being moved to the new Winter Palace. In 1755 tsarina Elisabeth of Russia (1741–62) had the amber panels moved south of St Petersburg to their final destination, the Catherine Palace at Tsarskoye Selo, where the room intended for them was considerably larger than the chamber in Berlin. The court architect Carlo Rastrelli (1700–71) was given the task of installing the Amber Room and he engaged an Italian, Martelli, and five amber craftsmen from Königsberg to carve more amber panels. By 1763 they had created a resplendent

King Frederick I of Prussia
(reigned 1701–13)

Tsar Peter the Great of Russia
(reigned 1682/89–1725)

The historic
Amber Room,
as it was in 1938.

The Catherine Palace in Tsarskoye Selo, where the Amber Room was from 1755–1942

room in which the original panels alternated with twenty-four Venetian mirrored rectangular columns resting on amber bases. A mirror, mounted in amber, a gift to tsarina Elisabeth from king Frederick II, had also been incorporated in the design. Additionally, four Florentine mosaics embellished the amber walls and gilded rocaille and other carved ornamentation adorned the white doors, while the floor was inlaid with mother-of-pearl, successfully uniting Baroque elements and complementary Rococo features.

After the tsarina Catherine II (1762–96), it was mainly 19th-century society that most admired the Amber Room. A British diplomat described it as the 'eighth wonder of the world', while the chamberlain Friederike Roltsch wrote: "The value of the Amber Room is incalculable." A dark chapter in the story of the Amber Room opened on 22 June 1941, the day Hitler launched Operation Barbarossa, the invasion of the Soviet Union. That same year, German soldiers stormed the opulent rooms of the Catherine Palace. Hans Hunsdörfer, a 'Wehrmacht' captain, described events: "Then I entered the Amber Room, where the walls were covered with thick cardboard. I saw two privates, keen to see what lay behind it, trying to tear down the protective covering. I intervened when they raised their bayonets in an attempt to prize off some mementos.

Come the next day, the Amber Room had been ravaged." An article in Berlin's *Lokal-Anzeiger* of 12 April 1942 read as follows: "An engineer and six privates carefully dismantled the panels over a period of 36 hours and crated them. Dr. Gall, the director general of Berlin's state palaces and gardens, then had them transported to the palace at Königsberg." The room intended for them there was too small, however, so that the mirrored columns had to be stored in the basement. Until the spring of 1944, the public was again able to view the Amber Room, albeit in a reduced format. Then, on 27 and 29 August 1944, Königsberg was bombed in allied air-raids and the palace burned to the ground. The Amber Room has now been lost, although its fate has never been established beyond doubt because of contradictory testimonies. Did the Amber Room fall victim to the flames? Was it evacuated in whole or in part? Is it lying in a warehouse in Weimar or Jonastal? The Russians at any rate have abandoned their search for it and have decided instead to rebuild it under the supervision of Professor Alexander Kedrinski and Alexander Shurawljow. Until new facts emerge in the story of the Amber Room, we can only agree with the closing words of German author Heinz G. Konsalik's 1986 novel, *Das Bernsteinzimmer* (The Amber Room): "It's gone, the Amber Room. The walls made of 'sun stone' have ceased to shine and only the sun that made them sparkle knows their fate. But the sun's not saying."

Giving up the search for the lost original: Russian workers during
the reconstruction of the north wall of the legendary Amber Room

Parts of the reconstructed Amber Room were shown at an exhibition
in Dortmund, Germany: left is a Prussian eagle in the panelling
of the room that one sees on the right with a console table.

Jewels and Treasures

A visit to the Green Vault of Dresden

"And though we might permit it to happen that the jewels and treasures in the famed Green Vault be shown to strangers and locals, a distinction must be made that not all and every one nor ever too many at once be conducted thither ..."

Decree by King Augustus the Strong, 1732

The ruling courts of Europe stared with astonishment towards Dresden when Augustus the Strong (1670–1733), Elector of Saxony and King of Poland, opened the Green Vault to all classes. For the first time, local and foreign nobility, merchants and scholars and, indeed, anyone of whatever origin and occupation were permitted to set foot within a royal treasury. Of course, every visitor had to report to the Elector's chief chamberlain and, upon payment of a ducat, received a pass for the visit. Thus the 'Privy Repository of the Green Vault' in the west wing of the Dresden palace became the first public museum of applied art. The Green Vault contained art collectors' and gem-cutters' pieces as well as natural curiosities, such as stuffed animals and bones, corals and ores, minerals and crystals. Since 1560, when Augustus I (reigned 1553–86) first set up his princely *Kunstkammer* (art collection), the electors of Saxony had endeavoured to build up a universal collection.

The tour started with the exhibits in the bronze and ivory rooms and then the silver and gilt silver room. Visitors were lost for words when they reached the room

The Obeliscus Augustalis in the Jewel Room of the Green Vault, as photographed in 1933.

filled with precious objects. In the environs of the Zwinger, the architect Matthäus Daniel Pöppelmann's architecture and the lime green-coloured capitals by court sculptor Benjamin Thomae, which gave the 'Privy Repository' vault the name it still bears, visitors could gaze upon numerous vessels made of varieties of jasper, or of agate, chalcedony, alabaster, lapis lazuli and serpentine, plus works of amber and rock crystal. The showpiece 'Royal Household on the Birthday of the Great Mogul Aurangzeb' (1701–08) – a joint work by court goldsmith Johann Melchior Dinglinger and his brother and enamelist Georg Friedrich – was found particularly impressive. This masterpiece of European jewellers' art is decorated with nearly 5,000 diamonds, 160 rubies, 164 emeralds and a sapphire. The legendary oriental splendour of the contemporary Great Mogul of India, Aurangzeb, is here combined with absolutist ideals to create a fairy-tale, courtly world.

Following the precious objects came a corner cabinet displaying miniature figures of pearls, sapphires, emeralds, ivory and enamelled gold, plus an armorial room with vessels of precious stones and ruby glass, as well as panelling with gilt armorial devices.

The last item in the tour through the Green Vault was the jewel room. Its furnishings surpassed everything that contemporaries had seen hitherto. Besides the coronation insignia of the Saxon and Polish royal house, the Wettin treasury, the principal works of the Dinglinger brothers

Royal church (Hofkirche) and Elector's palace in Dresden, in the west wing of which the Green Vault was housed until 1942.

Detail of the Obeliscus Augustalis, the principal item in the Green Vault, with the portrait of King Augustus the Strong. It is made of jasper, carnelian, diamonds, gems and cameos. The artists were Johann Melchior Dinglinger, Christoph Hübner and Christian Kirchner.
1719–22, Green Vault, Dresden

Throne area, Royal Household on the Birthday of the Great Mogul Aurangzeb, decorated with 5,000 precious stones. Johann Melchior and Georg Friedrich Dinglinger, 1701-1708, Green Vault, Dresden

also shone here in all their glory, glowing in the light of numerous candles. They included the memorial piece 'Obeliscus Augustalis'. In the words of the inventory: "The 'Obeliscus Augustalis' ... consists of all kinds of precious stones and also other oriental and rare stones. ... The portrait of His Royal Majesty stands on a pedestal set about with many diamonds and displaying the royal crown and elector's cap." The valuable stones and programmatic presentation of the 'Obeliscus Augustalis' were intended to exalt Augustus the Strong and place him on a level with the rulers of antiquity. Their marbled jasper tombs adorn the base, their green jasper cameos the shaft of the obelisk. The large cameo of Saxon jasper in the centre of the pedestal with the scene of the Trojan hero, Prince Hector, his wife, Andromache, and his son Scamandrius alludes to the future political deeds of the Saxon royal couple and the early death of their son.

The 'Moor with Rock Emeralds' was another piece in the jewel room that greatly attracted the interest of museum visitors. The figure is an inspired combination of mineralogical rarity with outstanding goldsmith, stone-cutting and sculptural work. The rock emeralds probably came from the Inca mines around Chivor and Somondoco in Colombia and, to the Spanish conquistadors, represented the very essence of 'West Indian' wealth. In 1581, the emperor Rudolph II presented this wonder of nature to the Elector August I. His successor, Augustus the Strong, was ill-satisfied with the original setting and therefore commissioned his court sculptor, Balthasar Permoser, to carve an Indian (wrongly described as a 'moor') of pear wood which would highlight the South American origin of the rock emeralds. The figure was subsequently painted dark brown by Martin Schnell. The Dinglinger workshop went to great trouble to render the body adornment of the Indian accurately. This included costly neck and arm bands, breastpieces and crown of plumes, loin-cloth and footwear of gilt silver, which the court jewellers mounted with rubies, emeralds, topazes, Ceylonese sapphires and garnets. Finally, the pedestal and bowl for the rock emeralds were designed by Wilhelm Krüger and coated with tortoiseshell veneer.

Johann Melchior Dinglinger with his Diana bowl.

Portrait of the Saxon royal sculptor Balthasar Permoser, by Adam Mányoki. Oil on canvas, c. 1710/15. Heimathaus, Traunstein

Permoser may have been inspired by the physiognomy of two South American princes bought by his royal patron and displayed to his amazed subjects.

From 1723, Augustus the Strong embarked on a construction programme for the Green Vault, furnishing it with unparalleled lavishness. The aim of this was to raise his political prestige in the eyes of high-born guests, flaunt the economic strength of his territories and emphasise the exportable nature of Saxon artistic handiwork and Saxon precious stones and minerals alike. In 1732, for example, the famed Schneckenstein locality in Saxony (mainland Europe's only source of topaz) provided Augustus the Strong with the raw material for many precious articles. In 1793, the Saxon poet Gotthelf Friedrich Oesfeld wrote in praise of it:

"Admire, wanderer, unique in Saxony / The cavernous vault of rock / In whose bosom nature shaped the growing topaz / In many a wondrous druse."

Moor with Rock Emeralds, decorated with emeralds, rubies, sapphires, topazes and garnets. Made by Balthasar Permoser jointly with the Dinglinger workshop, Wilhelm Krüger and Martin Schnell, pre-1724. Green Vault, Dresden

Theft, Murder and Death

For the sake of a diamond

"The most highly valued of human possessions, let alone gemstones, is the 'adamas' (which for long was known only to kings, and to very few of them). Indeed, the hardness of 'adamas' is indescribable, and so too that property whereby it conquers fire and never becomes heated. Hence it derives its name, because, according to the meaning of the term in Greek, it is the 'unconquerable force'."

Pliny the Elder, *Natural History*, in 10 volumes

Although today a diamond's value is solely determined by the "4 C's" – carat, colour, clarity, and cut – its magic remains undiminished. The diamond's extraordinary qualities, described by the Roman scholar Pliny the Elder (23–79), continue to fascinate.

According to an ancient Indian legend, the 'Koh-i-Noor' (108.93 carat), the 'Mountain of Light', was worn five thousand years ago by the hero Karna, son of the Sun God. Later it was revered by the moguls of India as a symbol of power and authority, until Delhi was plundered in 1739 by Persian Shah Nadir, who carried it off as war booty together with the diamond known as 'Darya-i-Noor' (186 carat), the 'Sea of Light'. In 1850, it was sent to England, as a gift to Queen Victoria, where it graces the crown of Queen Elizabeth II today.

At the very latest since the time of Alexander the Great, diamond octahedrons and oil-bound diamond powder were shipped from Old India to Europe for use as abrasives. During the Middle Ages, diamonds were believed to possess unlimited powers. Bishop Albertus Magnus of Regensburg (*c.* 1193–1280) described these as follows: "Magicians say that the diamond gives power over enemies when tied to the left upper arm. Its powers offer protection against insanity, wild animals and cruel people, disputes and quarrels." Charles the Bold shared this belief when he took the yellowish-green 'Florentine' (137 carat) into battle against the confederates. But the duke of Burgundy was defeated in the Battle of Grandson (2 March 1476) and lost his Indian diamond rose, cut into nine facets, which was later named the 'Florentine' after the de Medici family. In the autumn of 1476, Charles the Bold prepared for battle once again, taking with him another Indian diamond, the 'Sancy' (55 carat). This time the diamond brought even less luck. The Lorraines and the confederates were victorious and Charles was killed in the Battle of Nancy on 5 January 1477. A Swiss soldier stole the diamond from the fallen duke and sold it. By a circuitous route the diamond fell into the hands of the French nobleman Nicolas Harlay de Sancy, after whom it was subsequently named. De Sancy's servant tried to steal

Duke Charles the Bold of Burgundy,
who recklessly trusted in the
power of diamonds at the battles
of Grandson and Nancy.
Portrait by Rogier van der Weyden,
c. 1460

The Battle of Grandson,
from the chronicle by Werner Schodoler.
Pen-and-ink drawing, 1514,
Aarau, Canton Library

The Florentine, a replica by master stone polisher Rudolf Dröschel of Idar-Oberstein. The whereabouts of the original diamond, first seen by merchant and jeweller Jean Baptiste Tavernier on his journey to India in 1657, is not known.

the jewel, but was attacked and murdered. De Sancy retrieved his possession from the stomach of his domestic.

In the modern age, Europeans continued to buy rough diamonds from India. Jean Baptiste Tavernier, who bought the 'Brunswick Blue' (13.75 carat) and the 'Hope' (45.52 carat) in 1642, sold both to Louis XIV of France and was elevated into nobility for the service. The lustrous blue 'Hope' diamond, which the Sun King had cut, brought the monarch, his descendants and later owners little joy. Louis XIV's war fortunes deserted him. His nephew died. Louis XVI and Marie Antoinette ended on the guillotine. Princess de Lamballe was beaten to death during the French Revolution and her husband beheaded.

In 1830, the British banker T. H. Hope acquired the 'Hope' at auction for £18,000. Shortly afterwards, his son was the victim of poisoning. In 1900, the diamond was bought by the Turkish Sultan Abdul Hamid II for his favourite wife, who fell into the hands of murderers. Another owner of the 'Hope' is said to have been on board the Titanic when it sank in 1912. Finally, the fateful stone was bought by the diamond dealer Harry Winston for

US $179,920 and presented to the Smithsonian Institution in Washington, D.C.

Around 1700, the Venetian Vencento Peruzzi developed what is known as 'threefold goods', the round brilliant cut with 56 facets and one face that is common today, and which replaced the Mazarin cut, or 'twofold goods', with 32 facets. At the same time, a slave in the Indian Patriteal mine discovered the 'Regent' diamond (140.5 carat). He smuggled the diamond out of the mine in a wound dressing and offered it to an English sailor, who killed the slave and sold the stone. Through Thomas Pitt, governor of Fort George, the 'Regent' reached France in 1717 and came into the hands of the Bourbons. From 1804 onwards it graced the sword of Emperor Napoleon I and is now housed in the Louvre as one the most important diamonds in the history of France.

The 'Eugénie' (51 carat), on the other hand, was presented by Catherine the Great of Russia to Prince Grigory Potemkin for his services in 1762. His descendants sold the jewel to Napoleon III as a pendant for his bride, Eugénie de Montijo. After the Emperor's abdication, Mulhar Reo, then one of the richest men in the world, purchased the gemstone. But he disappeared in the aftermath of a lawsuit and with him, three of the historically most important diamonds, the 'Eugénie', the 'Star of the South' and 'English Dresden' (76.5 carat).

The latter hailed from Brazil, where diamonds were first discovered in 1721, as did the 'Maximilian' (33 carat), which was named after the Emperor of Mexico who was executed in 1867.

A number of new diamond sites were discovered only in the nineteenth century: in the Urals (1829), the United

Queen Elizabeth II on Coronation Day, 1953, with the Imperial State Crown and royal sceptre

States (1843), Australia (1852), South Africa (1866), China (1870) and Venezuela (1883). And knowledge of diamond properties also increased: thus French chemist Antoine Laurent Lavoisier (1743–94) succeeded in transforming a diamond into gaseous carbon dioxide through a heating experiment, while mineralogist Friedrich Mohs (1773–1839) defined the hardness scale, assigning the highest degree of hardness (10) to diamonds, and Scotsman James Ballantyne Hannay successfully produced the first synthetic diamond in 1880. Nevertheless, the search for natural gemstones continued, as in the Premier Mine in South Africa, where Frederick Wells discovered the largest rough diamond in the world on 26 January 1905, the 'Cullinan', with 3022 carat. The then government of Transvaal presented the stone to King Edward VII, who commissioned the I. J. Asscher and Company of Amsterdam to cut the 'Cullinan' into 105 polished diamonds. The nine largest remained in the possession of the English crown and the private property of the British royal family, including the 'Cullinan I', the largest polished diamond in the world with over 530 carat. Named the 'Great Star of Africa' by King Edward VII, it is today imbedded in the royal scepter; the 'Cullinan II', (317.4 carat) called the 'Second Star of Africa', on the other hand, graces the Imperial State Crown.

Despite its history of suffering, doom and death, in Buddhism the diamond is still considered a symbol of ultimate achievement.

The Cullinan I (replica by Rudolf Dröschel) is now on the sceptre of the English crown jewels.

The Imperial State Crown of Queen Elizabeth II, with the Cullinan II diamond on the circlet. Tower of London

Iridescent with a Hundred Lovely Colours

Precious stones in poetry of the modern era

The stone was an opal iridescent with a hundred lovely colours, and had the secret power to render pleasing to God and man anyone who wore it in this belief.

G. E. Lessing, *Nathan der Weise*, 1779

Poets, playwrights and artists of every age since the Baroque period – but particularly the Romantics – have been fascinated by stones and crystals. On a journey through the Alps, for example, the poet and natural philosopher Albrecht von Haller (1708–77) was particularly impressed by the sparkling crystals he saw. In his work on the Alps (1729), he boasts: "O wealth of

nature! Admit defeat, ye Latin dwarves. Europe's diamond blossoms here and grows into mountains." In his play *Nathan der Weise*, Gottfried Ephraim Lessing (1729–1828) considered that only the opals of triple rings could adequately indicate how important practical humanity was to the three great religions: Islamic, Jewish and Christian.

The Romantic poet Novalis (1772–1801) and the literary critic and Shakespeare translator Friedrich von Schlegel (1772–1829) were similarly enthusiastic about rock crystal. While in his novel *Heinrich von Ofterdingen* (1802) the former created cities, buildings and squares with crystal plants as Utopian living spaces, the latter recalls, via the example of the unfinished Cologne cathedral, the way the light is refracted by rock crystal.

In *Bergwerke zu Falun* (Mines of Falun) by E. T. A. Hoffmann (1776–1822), the protagonist succumbs to the fascination of the subterranean world of minerals and dies there, only to be resurrected as a spirit who seduces the living into yielding to the same fatal obsession. The love poems in the *West-östlicher Divan* by Goethe (1749–1832) draw on the qualities of precious stones attributed to them in the Orient: a carnelian talisman confers happiness and prosperity on the believer, an emerald makes a woman's finger look delightful, rubies and turquoises act as symbols of oriental opulence.

In his *Fall of the House of Usher* (1839), Edgar Allan Poe (1809–49) uses images of precious stones to convey the eerie aura of a ghostly palace: "And all with pearl and ruby glowing/ Was the fair palace door, / Through which came flowing, flowing, flowing / And sparkling evermore / A troop of Echoes …" In his poetry, hyacinth and agate feature in descriptions of female beauty, while diamonds are used to describe the graven images of sunken cities and tell of the petrified tears of fallen warriors.

Adalbert Stifter (1805–1868) makes rather different use of rocks, specifically granite, limestone, tourmalin,

Night, a copper engraving by Philipp Otto Runge.
Goethe Museum, Frankfurt/Main, 1802.
Inorganic nature is seen here in the form of crystals with a sunflower growing from them. This symbolises the glory of daytime, while the poppy above it represents sleep and dreams.

A valuable black opal from Lighting Ridge, Australia (29.6 carat). Ernst Schlangenotto Collection

rock crystal and katzensilber (biotite) in his tales *Bunte Steine* (Coloured Stones, 1853). They serve as titles for stories focusing on children, stories highlighting the harmony of nature and mankind from a cosmic point of view. In the novella *Bergkristall* (Rock Crystal), for example, Stifter's rocks convey the laws of nature, which find a parallel in human morality.

French writers also had their devotees of minerals and crystals, particularly their powers of attraction. Notable in this respect are the 19th-century symbolist poets Charles Baudelaire (1821–67) and the gem-obsessed Stéphane Mallarmé (1842–98).

Your Majesty Shall be Pleased

Peter Carl Fabergé, court jeweller to the tsars

"This work approaches perfection. It signifies the transformation of a jewel into a true objet d'art. Fabergé's work is characterized by flawless execution, complemented by precise settings, a quality that is amply evident in the miniature copies of the crown insignia of the Russian Imperial House, set with four thousand gemstones."

Rapport du Jury International (Joaillerie), 1902

Peter Carl Fabergé (1846–1920) and his firm gained worldwide acclaim following the World Fair in Paris in 1900. His business acumen and clever sales methods helped to establish this fame. "We always strive to present a large number of newly invented articles."

Fabergé's interest in gemstones was awakened during his travels to the three European gem-cutting centres: Florence, Dresden and Idar-Oberstein. He preferred to work with minerals from the Urals, the Caucasus and Siberia. Following his personal tastes, he mostly used nephrite, bowenite, chalcedony, agate, red jasper, lapis lazuli, mountain crystal, smoky quartz, obsidian and aventurine.

He was particularly admired by Queen Alexandra of England for his carved animals; her love of animals led to the famous collection in Buckingham Palace, London. Fabergé was inspired by the stone carving tradition of Saxony and Japanese netsuke in the creation of his stone animals, carved in one piece from agate and set with diamond eyes. He carefully selected matching minerals to make his carvings of animals as true to nature as possible. This phenomenon is even more evident in Fabergé's flowers in the treasuries at Vienna and St Petersburg. Using a *trompe l'oeil* technique, the blossoms were intended to enchant their wealthy owners during the long winter months in Russia. His caricaturist, folkloristic genre and portrait figures were used as table decorations and similar in style to the Russian porcelain figures from Moscow's Gardner porcelain manufacture.

True fame ultimately came to Peter Carl Fabergé, who had been promoted to the position of court goldsmith, in 1885, for his royal Easter eggs. In the year of Fabergé's appointment to court, the tsar Alexander III – following a Russian Orthodox tradition – presented his wife, Marie Feodorovna, with the first Fabergé egg adorned with a crown set with rubies and diamond rosettes. The gift was enthusiastically received and for each ensuing Easter feast Fabergé had to create an egg with a surprise centre. Even during the rule of the last tsar, Nicholas II, Peter Carl Fabergé or his son Eugène (1874–1960) continued to present their Easter eggs every year. Any attempts by the tsar to uncover the secret of following year's egg were always tactfully discouraged with the comment: "Your Majesty shall be pleased."

In 1913 – the anniversary year of the Romanov dynasty – Fabergé reached yet another highpoint with the creation of the 'Romanov 300th Anniversary Egg'. Four years later, the last royal Easter egg made of lapis lazuli could no longer be presented to the deposed tsar and his family. The House of Fabergé closed its doors in 1918. Peter Carl emigrated and died in Lausanne.

The name of Fabergé was not forgotten, however. Armand Hammer, an American entrepreneur and art collector, brought thirteen royal Easter eggs to the United States in 1925 and Emanuel Snowman of the firm Wartski acquired five of the tsarist bejewelled eggs – a collector's indulgence that would be close to impossible today.

Tsar Alexander III
was an avid gemstone collector

Peter Carl Fabergé
sorting precious stones

Top row, left to right: orange-tree egg with diamonds, citrine, amethyst, ruby and agate, 1911; lily-of-the-valley bouquet, with diamond flowers and nephrite leaves, 1896; bottom row, left to right: coronation egg with diamonds, ruby and rock crystal, 1897; mosaic egg with diamonds, ruby, emerald, topaz, sapphire and garnet, 1914

"Look on Me and Slumber"

Minerals in the 20th century

*Whenever you touch topaz, it touches you: it awakes
a gentle fire, like wine awakes in grapes. Still unborn,
clear wine seeks channels amidst the stone, demands
words, bestows its secret nourishment, shares out the kiss
of human skin: the touch of stone and man in serene peace
kindles garlands of fleeting flowers, which then return
to prime sources: flesh and stone: contrary elements.*

Pablo Neruda, *El topacio*

"Look on me and slumber" is how the Nobel
prize-winning Chilean poet Neftali Ricardo
Reyes, known as Pablo Neruda (1904–1973),
described an encounter with an imperial topaz, the trade
name for a topaz variety from a source near the Brazilian
city of Ouro Preto. In deep communion with the beauty
of nature, he dedicated two poems to the precious stone.
The play of sunny yellow light from the imperial topaz
reminded him of frozen honey, a day of gold or the wheat
of heaven.

Neruda is not alone among contemporaries fascinated
by the aura of minerals. Ever since Rudolf Steiner
(1861–1925) established a relation between mankind
and the spiritual principal of the cosmos in his doctrine
of anthroposophy and described precious stones as the
sensory organs of higher spiritual beings, precious stones
have played a fundamental role in esoteric thought.

In the meantime, mineralogists and biophysicians
alike have been hard at work in an endeavour to decode
the mysterious forces of minerals and crystals in a more
scientific fashion. Investigations with a scanning tun-
nelling microscope (STM) can now prove that stones
are not self-contained at molecular level but, in fact, have
a reciprocal relationship with their environment. They
can transform light, absorb warmth and emit wave energy.
Alternative and even orthodox medicine is becoming
more and more interested in lithotherapy, which goes
back thousands of years. The use of sulphur baths and
rock-salt inhalation in thorn houses to alleviate respira-
tory illnesses is no longer doubted by anyone. Countless
bodies worldwide have joined the research project into
lithotherapy, in an endeavour to establish lithotherapy as
an acknowledged natural therapy by systematic, empirical
and scientific means. New discoveries are helping analyt-
ical lithotherapy, including the minerals purpurite (1905),
benitoite (1907), creedite (1916), brasilianite (1945),

The biggest rock crystal
group in the world.
Discovered in West Arkansas
in 1981, it weighs 7.8 metric
tonnes, and measures
10' x 6'7" (3 x 2 m).
Kristallmuseum, Riedenburg

Nobel prize-winning Chilean
poet Pablo Neruda was fascinated
by topaz.

sinhalite (1952), tugtupite (1957), gaspeite
(1966), sekaniaite (1968), cavansite (1973),
sugulithite (1976) or the recently discovered mondolite.

The world press vies for attention
whenever unusual new finds are made,
such as the discovery of the largest rock
crystal group in the world that had formed
eighty-two feet down at Blocker Lead Mine
no. 4 in West Arkansas. The huge quartz,
weighing 7.8 metric tons, was shipped
via New Orleans, the Gulf of Mexico,
the Atlantic and Bremerhaven to go on
display at the Munich Mineral Days Expo,
Europe's biggest specialist fair. It is now
housed in the Crystal Museum at Riedenburg, Bavaria.

Topaz crystal from
Ouro Preto, Brazil.
5.5 cm long, it was
found around 1890.
Museum für Naturkunde
der Humboldt Universität,
Berlin

Quoted Sources and further References

Page 8: JADE IS BEAUTY IN STONE

Sources

Yang, Yang: Die Entstehung der Jade-
kultur. In: Das alte China.
Menschen und Götter im Reich
der Mitte 5000 v.Chr.–220 n.Chr.,
ed. Roger Goepper, Munich 1995, 95,
101, 103.
Buch der Lieder. In: Konfuzius, ed. Volker
Zotz, Reinbek bei Hamburg 2000, 65.

Secondary Literature

Eckart, Wolfgang U.: Geschichte der
Medizin, 2. ed., Berlin/Heidelberg/
New York et al., 1994, 28.
Kropp, Michael: Chinesische Jade,
Material, Herkunft, Bearbeitung.
In: Faszination Edelstein. Aus den
Schatzkammern der Welt. Mythos,
Kunst, Wissenschaft, ed. Sybille
Ebert-Schifferer, Martina Harms,
Darmstadt 1992, 196–197.
Laufer, B.: A Study in Chinese Archaeo-
logy and Religion, Field Museum
of Natural History, Publication 154,
Chicago 1912.
Reid, Daniel P.: Chinesische Naturheil-
kunde, Vienna 1988, 10.
Schmitz, Michael: Die Jade. In: Faszination
Edelstein. Aus den Schatzkammern
der Welt. Mythos, Kunst, Wissenschaft,
ed. Sybille Ebert-Schifferer, Martina
Harms, Darmstadt 1992, 196.
Yang, Yang, Die Entstehung der Jade-
kultur. In: Das alte China, Menschen
und Götter im Reich der Mitte 5000
v.Chr.–220 n.Chr., ed. Roger Goepper, Munich 1995, 95–105.
Zhongguo Shehui Kexueyuan Kaogu
Yanjiusuo (ed.): Mancheng Hanmu
fajue baogao, Peking 1980, 139.

Page 12: ALMOST BEYOND THE REACH
OF THE GODS

Sources

Bernier François: Voyages de F. Bernier
contenant la description des Etats
du Grand Mogol, de l'Indoustan,
Du Royaume de Kachemire 1699.
Holst, Walter von: Steinkreisel, SteinInfos 8.
In: http://www.steinkreis.de/steine8.
htm, Stuttgart 1998, 5.
Strabo: Geographica, ed. A. Meineke I–III,
Lib. xv, Teubn. 1851/52.

Secondary Literature

Delahoutre, Michel: Indische Kunst,
Ursprung und Entwicklung, Munich
1996, 13.
Eckart, Wolfgang U.: Geschichte der
Medizin, 2. ed., Berlin/Heidelberg/
New York et al. 1994, 26.
Franz, Heinrich Gerhard: Das alte Indien,
Geschichte und Kultur des indischen
Subkontinents, Munich 1990,
108–109, 114, 125, 173.
Jarrige, Jean-François: Vorzeit und Indus-
kultur. In: Das alte Indien, Geschichte
und Kultur des indischen Subkonti-
nents, ed. Gerhard Heinrich Franz,
Munich 1990, 76–79.
Okada, Amina, Nou, Jean-Louis: Taj
Mahal, Munich 1993, 9, 31.
Prasanna Kumar Acharya: Architecture of
Manasara. In: Manasara Series Vol. IV,
New Delhi 1994, ch. 15, 179–215.
Stietencron, Heinrich von: Religionen.
In: Das alte Indien, Geschichte und
Kultur des indischen Subkontinents,
ed. Gerhard Heinrich Franz, Munich
1990, 177–178.
Stromer, Wolfgang von: Gutenbergs
Geheimnis. Von Turfan zum Karlstein.
Die Seidenstraße als Mittler der
Druckverfahren von Zentralasien nach
Mitteleuropa, Geneva 2000, 17–18.
Wild, Klaus Eberhard: Zur Geschichte der
Edelsteinbearbeitung. In: Im Strome
sein, heißt, in der Fülle des Lebens
stehen, Festschrift Adolf Grub, ed.
Gymnasium Birkenfeld, Birkenfeld
1997, 332, 341.
Wirth, Gerhard: Alexander der Große,
Reinbek bei Hamburg 1973, 55–56.
Woodward, Christine, Harding, Roger:
Edelsteine, trans. Berthold Jäger,
Markt Schwaben 1989/90, 117.

Page 16: IN THE MAGIC GARDEN
OF PRECIOUS STONES

Sources

Das Gilgamesch-Epos, trans.: Albert Schott,
9. plate, Stuttgart 1997, 73, 74, 78.

Secondary Literature

Furlani, Giuseppe: Das Gilgamesch-Epos.
In: Das Gilgamesch-Epos, ed. Karl
Oberhuber, Darmstadt 1977, 375.
Guhr, Andreas: Mythos der Steine, Macht
und Magie, Hamburg 1995, 28.
Hansen, Donald P.: Frühsumerische
und frühdynastische Flachbildkunst.
In: Der alte Orient, ed. Winfried Orth-
mann, Frankfurt am Main/Berlin/
Vienna 1985, 191–193.
Matouš, Lubor: Die Entstehung des
Gilgamesch-Epos. In: Das Gilga-
mesch-Epos, ed. Karl Oberhuber,
Darmstadt 1977, 368.
Moore, Henry, Laroche, Lucienne:
Mesopotamien, Wiesbaden 1975,
22–23.
Moortgat, Anton: Die Kunst des Alten
Mesopotamien, Sumer und Akkad,
Cologne 1982, 53–54.
Strommenger, Eva: Fünf Jahrtausende
Mesopotamien. Die Kunst von den
Anfängen um 5000 v.Chr. bis zu
Alexander dem Großen, Munich 1962,
ill. XIII, XIV, XVI.

Page 18: COVERED WITH LAPIS LAZULI

Sources

Hornung, Erik: Das Totenbuch der
Ägypter, Zurich/Munich 1979, 110,
138–139, 166, 207, 336, 353, 372.
Die Mahnworte des Ipuwer. In: Altägyp-
tische Dichtung, ed. Erik Hornung,
Stuttgart 1996, 79.
G. Plinius Secundus: Naturalis Historiae,
Liber XXXVII, ed. Roderich König,
Zurich 1994, 54–55, 88–89, 98–99.
Sinuhe: Flucht und Heimkehr. In: Altägyp-
tische Dichtung, ed. Erik Hornung,
Stuttgart 1996, 40.

Secondary Literature

Aldred, Cyril: Die Juwelen der Pharaonen, Munich/Vienna/Zurich 1972, 115–129.

Bennett, John: The Restoration Inscription of Tut'Ankhamen. In: Journal of Egyptian Archaeology, vol. 25, 1939, 8–15.

Brier, Bob: Der Mordfall Tutanchamun, trans. Wolfgang Schuler, 2. ed., Munich/Zurich 2000, 18–22, 132, 143–144, 180, 239, 287.

Freed, Rita E.: Schönheit und Vollkommenheit – Zur pharaonischen Kunst. In: Ägypten. Die Welt der Pharaonen, eds. Regine Schulz, Matthias Seidel, Cologne 1997, 235.

Guhr, Andreas: Mythos der Steine, Macht und Magie, Hamburg 1995, 19–22.

Klemm, Rosmarie, Klemm, Dietrich D.: Steine und Steinbrüche im Alten Ägypten, Berlin/Heidelberg/New York 1992, 199–223, 379.

Kolta, Kamal Sabri, Schwarzmann-Schafhauser, Doris: Die Heilkunde im Alten Ägypten. Magie und Ratio in der Krankheitsvorstellung und therapeutischen Praxis, Stuttgart 2000, 18, 140 (=Sudhoffs Archiv, Zeitschrift für Wissenschaftsgeschichte, eds. Peter Ilg, Menso Folkerts, Gundolf Keil, Fritz Krafft, Rolf Winau, vol. 42).

Nunn, John F.: Ancient Egyptian Medicine, London 1996, 146.

Page 22: "AND THE STONES SHALL BE WITH THE NAMES OF THE TWELVE CHILDREN OF ISRAEL"

Sources

Daniel 10, 6, 38.

Ester 1, 6.

Exodus 28, 15–21; 31, 1–5.

Ezechiel 28, 13.

Ijob 28, 6, 15–19.

Jesaja 54, 11–12.

G. Plinius Secundus: Naturalis Historiae, Liber XXXVII, ed. Roderich König, Zurich 1994, 54–55, 88–89, 98–99.

Secondary Literature

Bolman, J.: Die Edelsteenen uit den Bijbel, 1938.

Friess, Gerda: Edelsteine im Mittelalter, Hildesheim 1980, 8.

Guhr, Andreas: Mythos der Steine. Macht und Magie, Hamburg 1995, 29–31.

Hansmann, Liselotte, Kriss-Rettenbeck, Lenz: Amulett, Magie, Talisman. Das Standardwerk mit fast 1000 Abbildungen, Hamburg 1999, 37–38.

Harris, Roberta L.: Das Zeitalter der Bibel. Spurensuche auf heiligem Boden, trans. Peter Knecht, Düsseldorf 1995, 86–105.

Heltzer, Michael: Skarabäen und Siegel. In: Archäologie zur Bibel, Kunstschätze aus den biblischen Ländern, ed. Royal Ontario Museum, Mainz 1981, 309–313.

Keller, Werner: Und die Bibel hat doch Recht, Forscher beweisen die Wahrheit des Alten Testaments, Düsseldorf/Vienna/New York 1989, 272.

Klemm, Rosmarie, Klemm, Dietrich D.: Steine und Steinbrüche im Alten Ägypten, Berlin/Heidelberg/New York 1992, 199–223, 379.

Matthiae, Paolo: Ninive, Glanzvolle Hauptstadt Assyriens, Munich 1999, 102.

Negev, Avraham (ed.): Archäologisches Bibellexikon, Neuhausen-Stuttgart 1991, 110–112. Hebrew stone terms: AHLMA (=amethyst); BAREKT (=emerald); DAR (=mother-of-pearl); EKDACH (=mountain crystal); CHORCHOR (=ruby?); GABIS (=crystal); JAHALOM (=carbuncle, chalcedony, onyx?); JASPE (=jasper); KADKOD (=hyacinth); LESCHEM (=opal?); NOFECH (=malachite); ODEM (=sardonyx?); PITEDA (=chrysolite); RAMOT (=coral?); SCHAMIR (=diamond); SAPIR (=lapis lazuli); SCHEBO (=agate); SCHOHAM (=onyx?); SOHERET (=black marmor); TARSCHICH (=turquoise?).

Page 24: THE PRECIOUS STONES WE SO DESIRE

Sources

Agatharchides von Knidos: Über das Rote Meer, ed. Dieter Woelk, Bamberg 1966, 66–67.

Aristoteles: Meteorologie über die Welt, book III, ch. 6, eds. Ernst Grumach, Hellmut Flashar, vol. 12, Berlin 1974, 89.

Platon: Phaidon, ch. 59, ed. Friedrich Schleiermacher, Andreas Graeser, Stuttgart 1987, 84.

G. Plinius Secundus: Naturalis Historiae, Liber XXXVII, ed. Roderich König, Zurich 1994, 21.

Theophrastus: De Lapidibus, ed. D. E. Eichholz, Oxford 1965, 64–67.

Secondary Literature

Fuhrmann, Richard Jürgen: Granat, Mystik, Edelstein, Schmuck, Stuttgart 1983, 14.

Graeser, Andreas: Nachwort zu Platon, Stuttgart 1987, 101–106, 124.

Guhr, Andreas: Mythos der Steine, Macht und Magie, Hamburg 1995, 100

Wild, Klaus Eberhard: Zur Geschichte der Edelsteinbearbeitung. In: Im Strome sein, heißt, in der Fülle des Lebens stehen, Festschrift Adolf Grub, ed. Gymnasium Birkenfeld, Birkenfeld 1997, 332–333.

Woodward Christine, Harding Roger: Edelsteine, trans. Berthold Jäger, Markt Schwaben 1989/90, 92.

Page 26: THE CONCENTRATED GLORY OF THE WORLD

Sources

G. Plinius Secundus: Naturalis Historiae, Liber XXXVII, ed. Roderich König, Zurich 1994, ch. 1, 17, ch. 88, 66–69.

Secondary Literature

Fellmann Brogli, Regine: Gemmen und Kameen mit ländlichen Kultzentren. Untersuchungen zur Glyptik der ausgehenden römischen Republik und der Kaiserzeit, Bern/Berlin/Frankfurt am Main/New York/Paris/Vienna 1996.

Petrikovits, Harald von: Die Rheinlande in Römischer Zeit, Düsseldorf 1980, 57–63

Simon, Erika: Augustus. Kunst und Leben in Rom um die Zeitenwende, Munich 1986, 156–161.

Wellmann, M.: Die Stein- und Gemmenbücher der Antike. In: Quellen und Studien zur Geschichte der Naturwissenschaften und der Medizin, vol. 4, 1935, 86–149.

Zanker, Paul: Augustus und die Macht der Bilder, Munich 1987.

Page 28: "HER SHINING WAS LIKE UNTO A STONE MOST PRECIOUS"

Sources

Arethas: Commentarius in Apocalypsin. In: Patrologia Graeca, vol. 106, Oxonia 1840, column 771–774.

Johannes-Offenbarung 4, 2–3; 21, 11; 21, 18–20.

Haimo von Auxerre: Expositio in Apocalypsin. In: Opera Omnia. Patrologia Latina, ed. J.-P. Migne, vol. 117, Turnholti nd., column 1205–1207.

Hrabanus Maurus: Opera omnia. In: Patrologia Latina, ed. J.-P. Migne, vol. 111, Paris 1852, column 465–472.

Beda Venerabilis: Explanatio Apocalypsin. In: Opera Omnia. Patrologia Latina, ed. J.-P. Migne, vol. 93, Paris 1862, column 196–202.

Secondary Literature

Benesch, Friedrich: Apokalypse. Die Verwandlung der Erde. Eine okkulte Mineralogie, 2. ed., Stuttgart 1993, 171–319.

Diekamp, F.: Analecta patristica, 1938, 165–168.

Meier-Staubach, Christel: Edelstein-deutung. In: Faszination Edelstein. Aus den Schatzkammern der Welt. Mythos, Kunst, Wissenschaft, eds. Sybille Ebert-Schifferer, Martina Harms, Darmstadt 1992, 113–117.

Schmid, J.: Studien zur Geschichte des griechischen Apokalypsetextes, Munich 1955 (=Münchner Theologische Studien, 1. Ergänzungsband).

Seel, Otto (ed.): Der Physiologus. Tiere und ihre Symbolik, 5. ed., Zurich/Munich 1987, 46–48, 56–57, 62, 66–69.

Page 30: PORPHYROGENNETOI: BORN IN THE PORPHYRY HALL

Sources

Darrouzès, J. (ed.): Epistoliers Byzantines du Xe siècle, Paris 1960, 317–332.

Hetherington, Paul: Byzanz – Stadt des Goldes, Welt des Glaubens, Luzern 1982, 22, 36.

Karayannopulos, Johannes, Weiß, Günter: Quellenkunde zur Geschichte von Byzanz, 1982, 392–393.

Secondary Literature

Clauss, Manfred: Konstantin der Große und seine Zeit, Munich 1996, 14.

Ducellier, Alain: Byzanz, Das Reich und die Stadt, Frankfurt am Main/New York/Paris 1990, 594.

Lilie, Ralph-Johannes: Byzanz, Kaiser und Reich, Weimar/Vienna 1994, 199–200.

Kolb, Frank: Diocletian und die erste Tetrarchie. In: Untersuchungen zur antiken Literatur und Geschichte, ed. W. Bühler, P. Herrmann, O. Zwierlein, vol. 27, Berlin/New York 1987.

Makris, Georgios: Biographisches Kirchenlexikon, vol. IV, 1992, column 463–464.

Trost, Vera: Tinten und Tintenhörnchen. In: Schreibkunst, Mittelalterliche Buchmalerei aus dem Kloster Seeon, eds. Josef Kirmeier, Alois Schütz, Evamaria Brockhoff, Augsburg 1994, 139–140.

Yerasimos, Stéphane: Konstantinopel, Istanbuls historisches Erbe, Cologne 2000, 64–65.

Page 32: THE GARNET RECEIVES ITS FIERY LUSTRE

Sources

Agnello: Liber Pontificalis Ecclesiae Ravennatis, ed. Duchesne, vol. XXVIII, Paris 1983, 86–88.

Aristoteles: Meteorologie über die Welt, eds. Ernst Grumach, Hellmut Flashar, vol. 12, Berlin 1984.

Isidor von Sevilla: Etymologiarum sive orignum, ed. W. M. Lindsay, Oxford 1957, 1962, Liber XVI, ch. XIII.

G. Plinius Secundus: Naturalis Historiae, Liber XXXVII, Cap. XXV, ed. Roderich König, Zurich 1994, 70–71.

Secondary Literature

Fuhrmann, Richard Jürgen: Granat. Mystik, Edelstein, Schmuck, Stuttgart 1985, 14.

Herwig, Wolfram: Die Goten. Von den Anfängen bis zur Mitte des 6. Jahrhunderts. Entwurf einer historischen Ethnographie, 3. ed., Munich 1990, 52–65, 358–360.

Löwe, Heinz: Deutschland im fränkischen Reich, 7. ed., Stuttgart 1982, 22.

Nell Macfarlane, Katherine: Isidore of Seville's Treatise on the Pagan Gods, Washington 1978, 1–4.

Palol, Pedro de, Hirmer, Max: Spanien. Kunst des frühen Mittelalters vom Westgotenreich bis zum Ende der Romanik, Munich 1991, 21.

Palol, Pedro de, Ripoll, Gisela: Die Goten. Geschichte und Kunst in Westeuropa, Augsburg 1999, 21–23, 55, 62, 262–264, 300.

Schatzkammer der Deutschen. Aus den Sammlungen des Germanischen Nationalmuseums Nürnberg, ed. Germanisches Nationalmuseum Nürnberg, Nürnberg 1982, 23.

Schumann, Walter: Edle Steine, 2. ed., Munich/Vienna/Zurich 1993, 80.

Sharpe, William D.: Isidore of Seville. The Medical Writings. Publications of the American Philosophical Society, Philadelphia 1964, 6–8, 20.

Page 36: DEDICATED TO THE BASILICA OF MONZA

Sources

quoted after: Dannheimer, Hermann: Denkmäler bayerischer Frömmigkeit aus der Zeit der Agilolfinger und Karolinger. In: Torhalle auf Frauenchiemsee, ed. Hermann Dannheimer, 2. ed., Munich/Zurich 1981, 110.

Gregor der Große; Cognomento Magni. In: Opera Omnia. Patrologia Latina, ed. J.-P. Migne, vol. 76, Paris 1849, Cap. XLVII, column 82–83.

Paulus Diaconus: Historia Langobardorum, ed. L. Bethmann, G. Waitz, Monumenta Germaniae Historica Scriptores rer. Lang., Liber IV., 1878, 27.

Paulus Diaconus: Historia Langobardorum, ed. Amedeo Giacomini, Udine 1982.

Secondary Literature

Friess, Gerda: Edelsteine im Mittelalter. Wandel und Kontinuität in ihrer Bedeutung durch zwölf Jahrhunderte in Aberglauben, Medizin, Theologie und Goldschmiedekunst, Hildesheim 1980, 11.

Jarnut, Jörg: Geschichte der Langobarden, Stuttgart/Berlin/Cologne/Mainz 1982, 39–46.

Reiser, Rudolf: Die Agilolfinger, Pfaffenhofen 1985, 42–50.

Reindel, Kurt: Das Zeitalter der Agilolfinger (bis 788). In: Handbuch der bayerischen Geschichte, ed. Max Spindler, vol. 1: Das alte Bayern. Das Stammesherzogtum bis zum Ausgang des 12. Jahrhunderts, 2. ed., Munich 1981, 142.

Stockmeier, Peter: Theodolinde, Königin der Langobarden. In: Bavaria Sancta, vol. 3, (1973), 9–20.

Page 38: THE BLACK STONE FROM THE GARDEN OF PARADISE

Sources

Aristoteles: De lapidibus. In: Opera Omnia. Patrologia Latina, ed. J.-P. Migne, vol. 171, Paris nd., column 1758–80.

Belenickij, A. M. (ed.): Al-Biruni. Sobrani svedenij dlja poznanija dragocenno-stej, Leningrad 1963, 234–235.

Secondary Literature

Denffer, Ahmad von: Wallfahrt nach Mekka. Das Wichtigste über umra und hadsch, Munich 1987, 17, 29–30, 40, 55, 68 (=Schriftenreihe des Islamischen Zentrums Munich, no. 15).

Faroqhi, Suraiya: Herrscher über Mekka. Die Geschichte der Pilgerfahrt, Munich/Zurich 1990, 15–43.

Friess, Gerda: Edelsteine im Mittelalter. Wandel und Kontinuität in ihrer Bedeutung durch zwölf Jahrhunderte in Aberglauben, Medizin, Theologie und Goldschmiedekunst, Hildesheim 1980, 19–22.

Guhr, Andreas: Mythos der Steine. Macht und Magie, Hamburg 1995, 150.

Schipperges, Heinrich: Eine "Summa Medicinae" bei Avicenna, Zur Krankheitslehre und Heilkunde des Ibn Sīnā (980–1037), Berlin/Heidelberg/New York 1987, 7–35.

Strohmaier, Gotthard (ed.): Al-Bīrūnī. In den Gärten der Wissenschaft, Leipzig 1991, 221, 298.

Woodward, Christine, Harding, Roger: Edelsteine, trans. Berthold Jäger, Markt Schwaben 1989/90, 92.

Page 40: SPARKLING PRECIOUS STONES, SHINING AND BRIGHT

Sources

Alcuin: Opera Omnia. In: Patrologia Latina, ed. J.-P. Migne, vol. 100, Paris 1863, column 656.

Vita Desiderii episcopi Cadurcensis. In: Monumenta Germaniae Scriptores rer. Merov., vol. IV, 576.

Haimo von Auxerre: Expositio in Apocalypsin. In: Opera omnia. Patrologia Latina, ed. J.-P. Migne, vol. 117, Turnholti nd., column 1205.

Beda Venerabilis: Explanatio Apocalypsis. In: Opera omnia. Patrologia Latina, ed. J.-P. Migne, vol. 93, Paris 1862, column 197–198.

Hrabanus Maurus: De Universo Libri. In: Opera omnia. Patrologia Latina, ed. J.-P. Migne, vol. 111, Paris 1852, column 466.

Walafrid Strabo: Theologica. In: Opera omnia. Patrologia Latina, ed. J.-P. Migne, vol. 114, Paris 1879, column 748.

Secondary Literature

Althoff, Gerd: Otto III., Darmstadt 1996, 149–150.

Braunfels, Wolfgang: Die Welt der Karolinger und ihre Kunst, Munich 1968, cat. XXXIX.

Brunner, Herbert: Die Kunstschätze der Münchner Residenz, ed. Albrecht Miller, Munich 1977, 150.

Elbern, Victor H.: Liturgisches Gerät und Reliquiare. Funktion und Ikonologie. In: 799, Kunst und Kultur der Karolingerzeit. Karl der Große und Papst Leo III. in Paderborn, ed. Christoph Stiegemann, Matthias Wemhoff, vol. 3, Mainz 1999, 694–710.

Friess, Gerda: Edelsteine im Mittelalter. Wandel und Kontinuität in ihrer Bedeutung durch zwölf Jahrhunderte in Aberglauben, Medizin, Theologie und Goldschmiedekunst, Hildesheim 1980, 24–43.

Görich, Knuth: Kaiser Otto III. und Aachen. In: Europas Mitte um 1000, ed. Alfried Wieczorek, Hans-Martin Hinz, vol. 2, Stuttgart 2000, 786–791.

Klemm, Elisabeth: Codex Aureus von St. Emmeram. In: Thesaurus librorum, 425 Jahre Bayerische Staatsbibliothek, ed. Karl Dachs, Elisabeth Klemm, Wiesbaden 1983, 32.

Schumann, Walter: Edle Steine, 2. ed., Munich/Vienna/Zurich 1993, 44–45, 137.

Untermann, Matthias: "Opere mirabili constructa". Die Aachener "Residenz" Karls des Großen. In: 799, Kunst und Kultur der Karolingerzeit. Karl der Große und Papst Leo III. in Paderborn, ed. Christoph Stiegemann, Matthias Wemhoff, vol. 3, Mainz 1999, 152–173.

Weber, Caroline: Sogenannter Talisman Karls des Großen. In: Krönungen, Könige in Aachen – Geschichte und Mythos, ed. Mario Kramp, vol. 1, Mainz 2000, 237–238.

Page 44: WITH A SWORD IN HIS HAND

Sources

quoted after: Castro, Americo: Spanien. Vision und Wirklichkeit, Cologne/Berlin 1957, 142.

Beda Venerabilis: Anglo-Saxonis Presbyteri. In: Opera Omnia. Patrologia Latina, ed. J.-P. Migne, vol. 93, Paris 1862, 202.

Secondary Literature

Graf, Bernhard: Oberdeutsche Jakobsliteratur. Eine Studie über den Jakobuskult in Bayern, Österreich und Südtirol, Munich 1991, 35, 166–167 (=Kulturgeschichtliche Forschungen, ed. Dietz-Rüdiger Moser, vol. 14).

Graf, Bernhard: Auf alten Wegen Europa neu entdecken, Munich 1992, 50.

Graf, Bernhard: Auf Jakobs Spuren in Bayern, Österreich und in der Schweiz, Rosenheim 1993, 34.

Herbers, Klaus, Plötz, Robert: Nach Santiago zogen sie. Berichte von Pilgerfahrten ans "Ende der Welt", Munich 1996, 18–19.

Hildburg, W. L.: Medieval Spanish Enamels and their Relation to the Origin and the Development of Copper Champlevé Enamels of the Twelfth and Thirteenth Centuries, Oxford 1936, 23 ff.

Hoenerbach, Wilhelm: Islamische Geschichte Spaniens, Zurich/Stuttgart 1970, 152–188, bes. 164–168.

Noack-Haley, Sabine, Arbeiter, Achim: Asturische Königsbauten des 9. Jahrhunderts, Mainz nd. (=Madrider Beiträge, vol. 22).

Palol, Pedro de, Hirmer, Max: Spanien. Kunst des frühen Mittelalters vom Westgotenreich bis zum Ende der Romanik, Munich 1991, 21, 34–35, 40, 161–162.

Plötz, Robert: El Apostel Santiago el Mayor en la tradicion oral y escrita. In: Santiago. Camino de Europa, Culto y cultera en la peregrinación a Compostela, Santiago de Compostela 1993, 205–206.

Schlunk, H.: The Crosses of Oviedo. A Contribution to the Jewelry in Northern Spain in the Ninth and Tenth Centuries. In: The Art Bulletin, vol. XXXII, no. 2, New York 1950, 91 ff.

Page 46: "YOU SHOULD GATHER SAMPLES OF EACH KIND"

Sources

Cook, James: Entdeckungsfahrten im Pacific. Die Logbücher der Reisen 1768–1779, ed. Edwin Hennig, Nördlingen 1987.
quoted after: Gaertner, Hildesuse, Reinhard, Michael: Neuseeland, Munich/Lucerne 1989, 59.
quoted after: Weyer, Helfried: Neuseeland. Fototräume am schönsten Ende der Welt, Frankfurt am Main 1992, 39.

Secondary Literature

Fischer Joachim: Die Maori – Kultur und Gesellschaft in voreuropäischer Zeit. In: Neuseeland, ed. Andris Apse, Joachim Fischer, Cologne 1989, 65–71.
Schumann, Walter: Edle Steine, 2. ed., Munich/Vienna/Zurich 1993, 137.
Walker, Ranginui: Maori. In: Merian, Neuseeland, ed. Manfred Bissinger, Will Keller, Hamburg 1996, 50–55.
Wattie, Nelson, Gaertner, Hildesuse: Neuseeland, Munich 1994, 44.

Page 48: THE CALL OF THE WILD

Sources

Azteken-Codices Matritenses, Real Academia, fol. 1735v und 1785r.
quoted after: Morton, Chris, Thomas, Ceri Louise: Tränen der Götter. Die Prophezeiung der 13 Kristallschädel, Augsburg 2000, 294–295.

Secondary Literature

Colas, Pierre R., Voß, Alexander: Spiel auf Leben und Tod. Das Ballspiel der Maya. In: Maya. Gottkönige im Regenwald, ed. Eva Eggebrecht, Matthias Seidel, Cologne 2000, 186–191.
Gilbert, Adrian G., Cotterell, Maurice M.: The Mayan Prophecies, Element Books, Shaftesbury 1995, 141–142.
Haberland, Wolfgang: Das Hochtal von Mexiko. In: Glanz und Untergang des Alten Mexiko, ed. Arne Eggebrecht, Mainz 1986, 46–57.
Morrill, Sibley S., Bierce, Ambrose: Frederick Albert Mitchell-Hedges and the Crystal Skull, London 1972, 8–13.

Morton, Chris, Thomas, Ceri Louise: Tränen der Götter, Die Prophezeiung der 13 Kristallschädel, Augsburg 2000, 63–67, 161–162, 334, 392.
Taube, Karl: Die Götter der klassischen Maya. In: Maya. Gottkönige im Regenwald, ed. Eva Eggebrecht, Matthias Seidel, Cologne 2000, 262–277.
Wagner, Elisabeth: Schöpfungsmythen und Kosmographie der Maya. In: Maya. Gottkönige im Regenwald, ed. Eva Eggebrecht, Matthias Seidel, Cologne 2000, 286.

Page 52: SAINT FAITH, COME TO MY AID

Sources

Bernard d'Angers: Liber Miraculorum Sancte Fidis, ed. M. L'Abbé A. Bouillet, Paris 1897, 48.
Hrabanus Maurus: Opera omnia. Patralogia Latina, ed. H.-P. Migne, vol. 111, Paris 1852, column 472–474.

Secondary Literature

Bernoulli, C.: Die Skulpturen der Abtei Conques-en-Rouergue, Basle 1956, 16–18 (= Basler Studien zur Kunstgeschichte, vol. XIII).
Fillitz, Hermann: Das Mittelalter I, Berlin 1984, 163 (=Propyläen Kunstgeschichte, vol. 5).
Herbers, Klaus (ed.): Der Jakobsweg. Mit einem mittelalterlichen Pilgerführer unterwegs nach Santiago de Compostela, 4. ed., Tübingen 1991, 115–116.
Keller, Harald: Zur Entstehung der sakralen Vollskulptur in der ottonischen Zeit. In: Festschrift für Hans Jantzen, Berlin 1951, 71–91.

Page 54: THIS STONE IS THE LODESTAR OF ALL PRINCES

Sources

Albertus Magnus: Opera omnia, vol. V: Liber primus mineralium, Tractatus II: De lapidibus pretiosis et eorum virtutibus, ed. Auguste Borgnet, Paris 1840, ch. 13.
Haimo von Auxerre: Opera omnia. In: Patrologia Latina, ed. J.-P. Migne, vol. 117, Turnholti nd., column 1206.
Hrabanus Maurus: Opera omnia. In: Patrologia Latina, ed. J.-P. Migne, vol. 111, Paris 1852, column 470–472.

Beda Venerabilis: Opera omnia. In: Patrologia Latina, ed. J.-P. Migne, vol. 93, Paris 1862, column 198, 202.
Walther von der Vogelweide: Sprüche, Lieder. Der Leich. Urtext und Prosaübertragung, ed. Paul Stapf, Berlin/Darmstadt 1963, 12.
Walther von der Vogelweide: Gedichte, ed. Karl Lachmann, Hugo Kuhn, 13. ed., Berlin 1965, 117.

Secondary Literature

Decker-Hauff, Hansmartin: Die Reichskrone, angefertigt für Otto I. In: Herrschaftszeichen und Staatssymbolik, ed. Percy Ernst Schramm et al., vol. 2, Stuttgart 1955, 560–637.
Friess, Gerda: Edelsteine im Mittelalter. Wandel und Kontinuität in ihrer Bedeutung durch zwölf Jahrhunderte in Aberglauben, Medizin, Theologie und Goldschmiedekunst, Hildesheim 1980, 84–80.
Graf, Bernhard: Ansätze der Kunstbetrachtung in Theorie und Praxis am Beispiel der Deutschen Reichskrone. In: Museumspädagogik in neuer Sicht – Erwachsenenbildung im Museum, ed. Hildegard Vieregg, Marie-Louise Schmeer-Sturm, Jutta Thinesse-Demel, Kurt Ulbricht, vol. 1, Baltmannsweiler 1994, 166–184.
Klaar, Karl-Engelhardt: Sicherung und Pflege der Reichskleinodien in Nürnberg. In: Nürnberg – Kaiser und Reich, Ausstellung des Staatsarchivs Nürnberg, Neustadt an der Aisch 1986, 77–81.
Kugler, Georg Johannes: Die Reichskrone, 2. ed., Vienna 1986, 29.
Löwe, Heinz: Die Staufer als Könige und Kaiser. In: Die Zeit der Staufer, Geschichte – Kunst – Kultur, vol. III, Stuttgart 1977, 28–29.
Machilek, Franz: Die Heiltumsweisung. In: Nürnberg – Kaiser und Reich, Ausstellung des Staatsarchivs Nürnberg, Neustadt an der Aisch 1986, 57–70.
Nellmann, Eberhard: Philippe setze en weisen ûf. Zur Parteinahme Walthers für Philipp von Schwaben. In: Stauferzeit, Geschichte, Literatur, Kunst, ed. Rüdiger Krohn, Bernd Thum, Peter Wapnewski, Stuttgart 1978, 87–104.
Schuhmann, Günther: Die Reichsinsignien und Heiltümer. In: Nürnberg – Kaiser und Reich, Ausstellung des Staatsarchivs Nürnberg, Neustadt an der Aisch 1986, 57–49.

Schulze-Dörrlamm, Mechtild: Die Kaiser-krone Konrads II. (1024–1039). Eine archäologische Untersuchung zu Alter und Herkunft der Reichskrone, Sigmaringen 1991, 117–138 (die problematische, auf stilistischen Kriterien basierende Datierung von Schulze-Dörrlamm trifft nur für den Kronenbügel zu).

Trnek, Helmut: Die Reichskrone. In: Weltliche und Geistliche Schatzkammer, Bildführer, ed. Kunsthistorisches Museum Vienna, 2. ed., Salzburg/Vienna 1991, 148.

Wolf, G.: Der "Waise". Bemerkungen zum Leitstein der Viennaer Reichskrone. In: Deutsches Archiv, Jg. 41 (1985), 39 ff.

Wolfram, Herwig: Überlegungen zur Datierung der Viennaer Reichskrone. In: Mitteilungen des Instituts für Österreichische Geschichtsforschung, vol. 78, Vienna 1970, 84 ff.

Page 58: MIX WELL WITH WATER AND EGG YOLK

Sources

Compositones ad tingenda musica, Codex Carol. od. Luc. 490, Kapitularbibliothek, Lucca.

Haimo von Auxerre: Expositio in Apocalypsin. In: Opera Omnia. Patrologia Latina, ed. J.-P. Migne, vol. 117, Turnholti, nd., column 937–1220, bes. 1192.

Heraclius: De coloribus et artibus Romanorum, vol. III. In: Speculum, ed. J. C. Richards, vol. 15 (1940), 59.

Theophilus Presbyter, Schedula diversarum artium, ed. Albert Ilg, Vienna 1874, ch. XIV, 30–31, ch. XV, 32–33, ch. XXXV, 76–77, 80–81.

Secondary Literature

Doerner, Max: Die Technik. In: Hochromanische Wandmalereien in Regensburg, ed. Hans Karlinger, Munich 1920, 75–80.

Roosen-Runge, Heinz: Farbgebung und Technik frühmittelalterlicher Buchmalerei. Studien zu den Traktaten "Mappae Clavicula" und "Heraclius", 2 Bde., Munich 1967.

Roosen-Runge, Heinz: Buchmalerei. In: Farbmittel, Buchmalerei, Tafel- und Leinwandmalerei, Reclams Handbuch der künstlerischen Techniken, vol. 1, Stuttgart 1984, 59–123.

Stein, Heidrun: Die romanischen Wandmalereien in der Klosterkirche Prüfening, Regensburg 1987, 65 (= Studien und Quellen zur Kunstgeschichte Regensburgs, vol. 1).

Trost, Vera: Chemische anorganische Farbmittel. In: Schreibkunst. – Mittelalterliche Buchmalerei aus dem Kloster Seeon, ed. Josef Kirmeier, Alois Schütz, Evamaria Brockhoff, Augsburg 1994, 140–143.

Trost, Vera: Traktate, Werkstatt- und Musterbücher. In: Schreibkunst. Mittelalterliche Buchmalerei aus dem Kloster Seeon, ed. Josef Kirmeier, Alois Schütz, Evamaria Brockhoff, Augsburg 1994, 146–147.

Page 62: "A GODSEND AND A CURE"

Sources

Führkötter, A, (ed.): Das Leben der Hl. Hildegard, berichtet von den Mönchen Gottfried und Theoderich, 3. ed., Salzburg 1980, 72.

Hildegard of Bingen: Physica, vol. 4: De lapidibus. In: Opera Omnia. Patrologia Latina, vol. CXCVII, ed. Basler Hildegard Gesellschaft, Basle 1982.

Hildegard of Bingen: Naturkunde. Das Buch von dem inneren Wesen der verschiedenen Naturen in der Schöpfung, trans. P. Riethe, 4. ed., Salzburg 1989, 82.

Hildegard of Bingen: Scivias – Wisse die Wege. Eine Schau von Gott und Mensch in Schöpfung und Zeit, trans. Walburga Storch, 2. ed., Freiburg/Basle/Vienna 1996, 5–6.

Hildegard of Bingen: Heilkraft der Natur – "Physica". Rezepte und Ratschläge für ein gesundes Leben, trans. M.-L. Portmann, 3. ed., Freiburg/Basle/Vienna, 1997, 298, 303.

Marbod de Rennes: De lapidibus, ed. C. W. King und J. M. Riddle, Wiesbaden 1977.

Secondary Literature

Kotzur, H.-Jürgen (ed.): Hildegard von Bingen, Mainz 1998.

Saurma-Jeltsch, Liselotte: Die Miniaturen im Liber scivias der Hildegard von Bingen, Hamburg 1998.

Schiller, Reinhard: Hl. Hildegard. Atlas der Edelsteine und Metalle. Von Wirkung und Nutzen der Edelsteine und Metalle für die Gesundheit nach der

hl. Hildegard von Bingen, Augsburg 1993, 13–88.

Schipperges, Heinrich: Krankheitsursache, Krankheitswesen und Heilung in der Klostermedizin, dargestellt am Weltbild Hildegards von Bingen, dis., Bonn 1951.

Schipperges, Heinrich: Die Welt der Hildegard von Bingen, Freiburg im Breisgau 1997.

Page 66: IT CONFERS STRENGTH AGAINST ENEMIES

Sources

Albertus Magnus: De mineralibus. Opera omnia, ed. A. Borgnet, vol. V, Paris 1890, ch. 1.

Albertus Magnus: De mineralibus, ed. Günther Goldschmidt, Basle 1985, 14–15.

Secondary Literature

Engelen, Ulrich: Die Edelsteine in der deutschen Dichtung des 12. und 13. Jahrhunderts, Munich 1978, 297–311 (= Münsterische Mittclalter-Schriften, ed. Hans Belting et al., vol. 27).

Gillingham, John: Richard the Lionhcart, London 1978, 169–217.

Gillingham, John: Richard Löwenherz. Eine Biographie, Herrsching 1990.

Gillingham, John: Richard Coeur de Lion. Kingship, Chivalry and War in the Twelth Century, London 1994.

Gillingham, John: Richard I., New Haven 1999.

Kessler, Ulrike: Richard I. Löwenherz. König, Kreuzritter, Abenteurer, Graz/Vienna/Cologne 1995, 105–306.

Lloyd, Simon: Die Kreuzzugsbewegung 1096–1274. In: Illustrierte Geschichte der Kreuzzüge, ed. Jonathan Riley-Smith, Christian Rochow, Frankfurt am Main/ New York 1999, 46–82.

Milger, Peter: Die Kreuzzüge. Krieg im Namen Gottes, Augsburg 2000, 241–261.

Pernoud, Régine: Der Abenteurer auf dem Thron. Richard Löwenherz, König von England, Munich 1994, 99–236.

Woodward, Christine, Roger, Harding: Edelsteine, trans. Berthold Jäger, Markt Schwaben 1989/90, 25.

Page 68: ALL YOUR WALLS ARE OF PRECIOUS STONES

Sources

Suger von St-Denis: Liber de rebus in administratione sua gestis, Liber XXXIII.

Suger von St-Denis: Libellus de consecratione ecclesiae Sancti Dionysii, Liber VII, ed. Günther Binding, Cologne 1995 (=Veröffentlichung der Abteilung Architekturgeschichte des Kunsthistorischen Instituts der Universität Cologne, vol. 56).

Suger von St-Denis: Ausgewählte Schriften, ed. Andreas Speer, Darmstadt 2000.

Suger von St-Denis: Über den Neubau der Abteikirche in Saint-Denis. In: Die Gotik des Abendlandes. Idee und Wandel, ed. Hans Jantzen, Cologne 1962, 213–219.

Secondary Literature

Assunto, Rossario: Die Theorie des Schönen im Mittelalter, Cologne 1982, 194.

Gall, Ernst: Die gotische Baukunst in Frankreich und Deutschland, Leipzig 1925, 93ff.

Jantzen, Hans: Die Gotik des Abendlandes, Idee und Wandel, Cologne 1962, 42–62.

Panofsky, Erwin: Gothic Architecture and Scholasticism, 13. ed., Cleveland/ New York 1970.

Panofsky, Erwin: Abbot Suger on the Abbey Church of St-Denis and its Art Treasures, 2. ed., Princeton 1979.

Schäfke, Werner: Frankreichs gotische Kathedralen, Cologne 1979, 16–25.

Sedlmayr, Hans: Die Entstehung der Kathedrale, 2. ed., Graz 1976.

Page 70: "THIS STONE IS CALLED THE GRAIL"

Sources

Boron, Robert de: Joseph d'Arimathie, ed. Richard O'Gorman, Toronto 1995, 5–575.

Chrétien de Troyes: Perceval le Gallois ou Le conte du Graal, ed. Keith Busby, Tübingen 1993, vers. 2976–3690, 6217–6518 (cf. 12576, Bibliothèque Nationale, Paris).

Hartmann von Aue: Iwein, ed. Thomas Cramer, 3. ed., Berlin/New York 1981, 24, Vers 1202–1209.

Scharfenberg, Albrecht von: Der jüngere Titurel, ed. Werner Wolf, Kurt Nyholm, 5 Bde., Berlin 1955/92, Vers 324–580, 6172–6173, 6242ff.

Türlin, Heinrich von dem: Die Krone, ed. Alfred Ebenbauer, Fritz P. Knapp, Tübingen 2000, vers. 29367–29377, 29408–29429.

Wolfram of Eschenbach: Parzival, ed. Karl Lachmann, Wolfgang Spiewok, vol. 2, Stuttgart 1981, book 5, ch. 224–255, book 9, ch. 446–468, 469, vers. 3–28, 470–552, book 16, ch. 790–796.

Secondary Literature

Bonnet, Anne-Marie: Rodenegg und Schmalkalden. Untersuchungen zur Illustration einer ritterlich-höfischen Erzählung und zur Entstehung profaner Epenillustration in den ersten Jahrzehnten des 13. Jahrhunderts, Munich 1986, 26–30.

Ducluzeau, Francis: Le monde du Graal. Les racines initiatiques de l'imaginaire chevaleresque, Monaco 1997, 4–404.

Engelen, Ulrich: Die Edelsteine in der deutschen Dichtung des 12. und 13. Jahrhunderts, Munich 1978, 46, 66, 85–406, bes. 126 (=Münsterische Mittelalter-Schriften, ed. Hans Belting et al., vol. 27).

Kühbacher, Egon: Literatur und bildende Kunst im Tiroler Mittelalter. Die Iwein-Fresken von Rodenegg und andere Zeugnisse der Wechselwirkung von Literatur und Kunst, Innsbruck 1982, 10ff. (=Innsbrucker Beiträge zur Kulturwissenschaft, Germanistische Reihe, vol. 15).

Lincoln, Henry, Baigent, Michael, Leigh, Richard: Der Heilige Gral und seine Erben, 5. ed., Bergisch Gladbach 1986, 256–275.

Masser, Achim: Die Iwein-Fresken von Burg Rodenegg in Südtirol und der zeitgenössische Ritterhelm, Achim Masser zum 60. Geburtstag am 12. Mai 1993, Innsbruck 1993, 178–198.

Rasmo, Nicolo: Überraschende Funde. In: Merian, Südtirol, vol. 26, 9 (1974), 48ff., 100ff.

Schupp, Volker: Kritische Anmerkungen zur Rezeption des deutschen Artusromans an Hand von Hartmanns Iwein. In: Frühmittelalterliche Studien, vol. 9 (1975), 405ff.

Weddige Hilkert: Einführung in die germanistische Mediävistik, Munich 1997, 187–204.

Yerasimos, Stéphane: Konstantinopel. Istanbuls historisches Erbe, Cologne 2000, 8.

Page 74: AMONG THEM THERE IS EVEN CHALCEDONY

Sources

quoted after: Ambros, Eva (ed.): Venedig, Berlin/Gütersloh/Munich/Stuttgart 1988, 115.

quoted after: Calimani, Riccardo: Die Kaufleute von Venedig. Die Geschichte der Juden in der Löwenrepublik, trans. Sylvia Höfer, Düsseldorf 1988, 318.

Sabellico, Marc'Antonio: Del sito di Venezia città, Venezia 1502, Nachdruck: ed. G. Meneghetti, Venice 1957.

quoted after: Sammartini, Tudy: Stein böden in Venedig, Munich 2000, 31.

Secondary Literature

Brugger-Koch, S.: Venedig und Paris. Die wichtigsten Zentren des hochmittelalterlichen Hartsteinschliffs, Zeitschrift des Deutschen Vereins für Kunstwissenschaft, Munich 1985, 3–39.

Kramer, Joachim: Pfau. In: Lexikon der christlichen Ikonographie, ed. Günter Bandmann, Wolfgang Braunfels, Johannes Kollwitz, Wilhelm Mrazek, Alfred A. Schmid, Hugo Schnell, vol. 3, Rom/Freiburg/Basle/Vienna 1990, column 409–411.

Romanelli, Giandomenico (ed.): Venedig. Kunst & Architektur, Cologne 1997, 92–94.

Sammartini, Tudy: Steinböden in Venedig, Munich 2000, 115, 121, 180.

Sibylle, Eva, Rösch, Gerhard: Venedig im Spätmittelalter 1200–1500, Freiburg/ Würzburg 1991, 153, 206.

Wild, Klaus Eberhard: Zur Geschichte der Edelsteinverarbeitung. In: Im Strome sein, heißt, in der Fülle des Lebens stehen, Festschrift Adolf Grub, ed. Gymnasium Birkenfeld, Birkenfeld 1997, 337.

Page 78: TAINTED BY ORIGINAL SIN

Sources

Albertus Magnus: De mineralibus. Opera omnia, ed. A. Borgnet, vol. V, Paris 1890, 1–116.

Albertus Magnus: De mineralibus, ed. Günther Goldschmidt, Basle 1983, 14

Bartholomaeus Anglicus: De proprietatibus rerum, Basle 1470.

Konrad von Megenberg: Von den edelen stainen und des êrsten in ainer gemain. In: Edelsteinmedizin im Mittelalter. Die Entwicklung der spätantiken und mittelalterlichen Lithotherapie unter besonderer Berücksichtigung des Konrad von Megenberg, ed. Rainer A. Müller, Munich 1984, 81.

Meister Eckhart: Deutsche Predigten und Traktate, ed. Josef Quint, Munich 1968, 140.

Santa Teresa de Jesus: Primeras Moradas. In: Obras Completas, ed. Efren de la Madre de Dios, O. C. D. y Otger Stegginkk, O. Carm., Madrid 1986, ch. 1.

Teresa von Avila: Die innere Burg, ed. Fritz Vogelsang, Zurich 1979, 21–22.

Thomas von Chantimpré: Opus de natura rerum, ed. H. Boese, Berlin 1973.

Vinzenz de Beauvais: Speculum naturale. In: Speculum maius, vol. 1, Douai 1624.

Volmar: Das Steinbuch. Ein altdeutsches Gedicht, ed. Hans Lambel, Heilbronn 1877, 1–137.

Secondary Literature

Aerts, Willem J. (ed.): Vincent of Beauvais and Alexander the Great. Studies on the Speculum maius, Groningen 1986, 5–187.

Biedermann, Hans: Medicina magica. Metaphysische Heilmethoden in spätantiken und mittelalterlichen Handschriften, Graz 1972.

Fischer, Hanns, Janota, Johannes (ed.): Der Stricker. Verserzählungen, 2 Bde., 3. ed., Tübingen 1967/73.

Guhr, Andreas: Mythos der Steine. Macht und Magie, Hamburg 1995, 155.

Fühner, Hermann: Lithotherapie. Historische Studien über die medizinische Verwendung der Edelsteine, Ulm 1957.

Langosch, Karl, Stammler, Wolfgang: Die deutsche Literatur des Mittelalters, Verfasserlexikon, vol. IV, Berlin 1953, 717–718.

Martin, E.: Im Stein ist heilende Medizin und Magie in mittelalterlichen Steinbüchern. In: Die Grünthal-Waage, vol. 6, Stolberg 1967, 136–140.

Müller, Rainer A.: Edelsteinmedizin im Mittelalter. Die Entwicklung der spätantiken und mittelalterlichen Lithotherapie unter besonderer Berücksichtigung des Konrad von Megenberg, Munich 1984.

Riddle J. M.: Lithotherapy in the Middle Ages, Lapidaries Considered as Medical Texts. In: Pharmacy in History, vol. 12 (1970), 39–50.

Stahl, Peter (ed.): Peter Königschlachter: Das Buch von Naturen der Ding. Übersetzung des Liber de natura rerum des Thomas von Chantimpré, Würzburg 1987, 3–55.

Weber, Christian: Mittelalterliche Vorstellungen über Edelsteine und deren Kräfte. Volkskundliche Untersuchungen und Quellennachweise zu dem sechsten Hauptstück von Konrad von Megenbergs Buch der Natur, dis., Cologne 1939.

Page 80: "Your Diadem shall Shine"

Sources

Annales Stamensis, Additiones III, fol. 394r.

Karl IV.: Vita ab eo ipso conscripta, ed. C. Winter, Heidelberg 1950, 8.

Secondary Literature

Hillenbrand, E.: Die Autobiographie Karls IV., Entstehung und Funktion. In: Kaiser Karl IV. (1516–78), ed. H. Patze, Neustadt an der Aisch 1978, 39–72.

Kavka, F.: Am Hofe Karls IV., Stuttgart 1990, 146.

Legner, A.: Karolinische Edelsteinwände. In: Kaiser Karl IV., Staatsmann und Mäzen, ed. F. Seibt, 2. ed., Munich 1978, 356–362.

Machilek, F.: Privatfrömmigkeit und Staatsfrömmigkeit. In: Kaiser Karl IV., Staatsmann und Mäzen, ed. F. Seibt, 2. ed., Munich 1978, 87–101.

Poche, E.: Einige Anmerkungen über die Kameen Karls IV.. In: Sborník k sedmdesátinám Jana Kveta (1965), 84.

Rädle, F.: Karl IV. als lateinischer Autor. In: Kaiser Karl IV. Staatsmann und Mäzen, ed. F. Seibt, 2. ed., Munich 1978, 253–259.

Schneider, R.: Karls IV. Auffassung vom Herrscheramt. In: Historische Zeitschrift, Munich 1973, 122–150.

Seibt, Ferdinand: Karl IV. Ein Kaiser in Europa 1346 bis 1378, Munich 1985, 145–147.

Stromer, Wolfgang von: Gutenbergs Geheimnis. Von Turfan zum Karlstein. Die Seidenstraße als Mittler der Druckverfahren von Zentralasien nach Mitteleuropa, Geneva 2000, 10–11, 40–43.

Page 84: Cut and Polished

Sources

Heraclius: De coloribus et artibus Romanorum, vol. 1, ch. XII. In: Speculum, ed. J. C. Richards, vol. 15 (1940), 263–267.

G. Plinius Secundus: Naturalis Historiae, Liber XXXVII, ed. Roderich König, Zurich 1994, 21, 135.

Theophilus Presbyter: Schedula diversarum artium, vol. III, ch. 95, ed. A. Ilg, Vienna 1874, 354.

Secondary Literature:

Auzolle, Michel: Tableau généalogique des rois de France, Paris 1982, 5.

Bänsch, Birgit, Linscheid-Burdich, Susanne: Theophilus, Schedula diversarum artium: Textauszüge. In: Ornamenta Ecclesiae, Kunst und Künstler der Romanik in Cologne, ed. Anton Legner, vol. 1, Cologne 1985, 374.

Freise, Eckhard: Zur Person des Theophilus und seiner monastischen Umwelt. In: Ornamenta Ecclesiae. Kunst und Künstler der Romanik in Cologne, ed. Anton Legner, vol. 1, Cologne 1985, 357–361.

Pazaurek, Gustav E.: Mittelalterlicher Edelsteinschliff. In: Belvedere 9 (1930), 145–194.

Stromer, Wolfgang von: Modell der Edelstein-Schleifmaschine des Heinrich Arnold aus Zwolle von 1439. In: Faszination Edelstein. Aus den Schatzkammern der Welt. Mythos, Kunst, Wissenschaft, ed. Sybille Ebert-Schifferer, Martina Harms, Darmstadt 1992, 120–121.

Theobald, Wilhelm, Stromer, Wolfgang von (ed.): Technik des Kunsthandwerks im 12. Jahrhundert des Theophilus Presbyter. Diversarum artium schedula, Düsseldorf 1984, 173–174.

Wild, Klaus Eberhard: Zur Geschichte der neuzeitlichen Steinschneidekunst unter besonderer Berücksichtigung des Edelsteingraveurgewerbes in Idar-Oberstein, Heimat und Museum, Festschrift für Alfred Peth, Idar-Oberstein 1996, 68–87.

Wild, Klaus Eberhard: Zur Geschichte der Edelsteinbearbeitung. In: Im Strome sein, heißt, in der Fülle des Lebens stehen, Festschrift für Adolf Grub, ed. Gymnasium Birkenfeld, Birkenfeld 1997, 331–352.

Page 86: THE SPANISH AND THEIR 'WORTHLESS' TURQUOISE

Sources

Anónymo de Tlatelolco, 1528. In: Rückkehr der Götter. Aufzeichnungen der Azteken über den Untergang ihres Reiches, ed. Miguel León-Portilla, Renate Heuer, Zurich 1986, 115, 120.

Braun, Karl (ed.): "Sie suchen nach dem Gold wie Schweine". Die Eroberung Mexiko-Tenochtitlans aus indianischer Sicht. Zusammengestellt und übersetzt nach Bildern und Texten von Bernardino de Sahagún, Tübingen 1982, 66–67.

Codex Florentino, Buch XII. In: Rückkehr der Götter. Aufzeichnungen der Azteken über den Untergang ihres Reiches, ed. Miguel León-Portilla, Renate Heuer, Zurich 1986, 26–30, 49, 59–60, 64, 66–67, 70, 83, 99, 103–105.

De la venida de los espanoles y principes de la ley evangélica, realción XIII. In: Rückkehr der Götter. Aufzeichnungen der Azteken über den Untergang ihres Reiches, ed. Miguel León-Portilla, Renate Heuer, Zurich 1986, 108.

Tezozómoc, Alvarado: Crónica mexicáyotl, ch. CVI und CVII, A. 17. c. In: Rückkehr der Götter. Aufzeichnungen der Azteken über den Untergang ihres Reiches, ed. Miguel León-Portilla, Renate Heuer, Zurich 1986, 24–25.

Secondary Literature

Eggebrecht, Eva. "Ich und meine Gefährten leiden an einer Krankheit des Herzens, die nur mit Gold geheilt werden kann …". In: Glanz und Untergang des Alten Mexiko, ed. Arne Eggebrecht, Mainz 1986, 162–184.

Haberland, Wolfgang: Das Hochtal von Mexiko. In: Glanz und Untergang des Alten Mexiko, ed. Arne Eggebrecht, Mainz 1986, 58–86, bes. 63.

Hartau, Claudine: Hernando Cortés, Reinbek bei Hamburg 1994, 53, 77, 95.

Hugh, Thomas: Die Eroberung Mexikos. Cortés und Montezuma, trans. Thorsten Schmidt, Frankfurt am Main 1998, 229–250, 649–676.

König, Hans-Joachim: Die Entdeckung und Eroberung Amerikas, 1492–1550, Würzburg 1992, 104–144.

König, Viola: Die Hauptgottheiten. In: Glanz und Untergang des Alten Mexiko, ed. Arne Eggebrecht, Mainz 1986, 120–121.

Seler, E.: Einige Kapitel aus dem Geschichtswerk des Fray Bernardino de Sahagún, Stuttgart 1927, 376.

Zeuske, Max: Die Conquista, Leipzig 1992, 57–85.

Page 90: THE GARDEN OF HEALTH

Sources

Agrippa, Cornelius: De occulta philosophia libri tres, ed. Perrone Compagni, Leiden/New York/Cologne 1992, Chs. XXIII–XXIX, 131–142 (= Studies in the History of Christian Thought, ed. Heiko A. Oberman, vol. XLVIII).

Cube, Johann Wonnecke von: Hortus sanitatis, Mainz 1485, ch. CLXXIII.

Theophrast von Hohenheim: De mineralibus. In: Medizinische, naturwissenschaftliche und philosophische Schriften, ed. Karl Sudhoff, Munich/Berlin 1930, 31–63.

Secondary Literature

Benzenhöfer, Udo: Paracelsus, Reinbek bei Hamburg 1997, 7–139.

Fühner, H.: Lithotherapie. Historische Studien über die medizinische Verwendung der Edelsteine, Ulm 1957.

Goldammer, Kurt, Weimann, Karl–Heinz (ed.): Paracelsus. Vom Licht der Natur und des Geistes, Stuttgart 1993, 7–34, 144.

Martin, E.: Im Stein ist heilende Medizin und Magie in mittelalterlichen Steinbüchern. In: Die Grünthal-Waage, vol. 6, Stolberg 1967, 136–140.

Riddle J.M.: Lithotherapy in the Middle Ages. Lapidaries Considered as Medical Texts. In: Pharmacy in History, vol. 12 (1970), 39–50.

Rueb, Franz: Mythos Paracelsus: Werk und Leben von Philippus Aureolus Theophrastus Bombastus von Hohenheim, Berlin/Munich 1995, 47–61.

Schwedt, Georg: Paracelsus in Europa. Auf den Spuren des Arztes und Naturforschers 1493–1541, Munich 1993, 31–254.

Waldeck, Hans: Mineralien, Edelsteine, Medizin – kulturgeschichtliche Zusammenhänge. In: Faszination Edelstein. Aus den Schatzkammern der Welt. Mythos, Kunst, Wissenschaft, ed. Sybille Ebert-Schifferer, Martina Harms, Darmstadt 1992, 93–103.

Page 92: LOCKED IN THE VAULTS FOR EVER

Sources

Agricola, Georgius: De re metallica libri XII, trans. Georg Fraustadt, Hans Prescher, Berlin 1974, 53–723.

quoted after: Brunner, Herbert: Die Kunstschätze der Münchner Residenz, ed. Albrecht Miller, Munich 1977, 127.

Quiccheberg, Samuel à: Inscriptiones vel tituli theatri amplissimi complectentis rerum universitatis singulas materias et imagines eximias, Munich 1565.

Secondary Literature

Bauer, Reinhard, Piper, Ernst: München, Die Geschichte einer Stadt, Munich 1993, 101–102.

Benker, Sigmund: Die Kunstentwicklung vom 16. bis zum 18. Jahrhundert. In: Handbuch der Bayerischen Geschichte, ed. Max Spindler, Andreas Kraus, vol. 2, 2. ed., Munich 1988, 1058.

Hajos, E. M.: The concept of an engravings collection in the year 1565. In: The Art Bulletin, vol. 40 (1958), 151–156.

Lutz, Heinrich, Ziegler, Walter: Bayern als Vormacht der Gegenreformation. In: Handbuch der Bayerischen Geschichte, ed. Max Spindler, Andreas Kraus, vol. 2, 2. ed., Munich 1988, 387–392.

Seelig, Lorenz: Die Münchner Kunstkammer. Geschichte, Anlage, Ausstattung. In: Jahrbuch der Bayerischen Denkmalpflege, vol. 40, Munich 1989, 119–124.

Stierhof, Horst H.: Zur Baugeschichte der Maximilianischen Residenz. In: Wittelsbach und Bayern. Um Glauben und Reich. Kurfürst Maximilian I., Beiträge zur Bayerischen Geschichte und Kunst 1573–1657, Munich/Zurich 1980, 269.

Syndram, Dirk: Die Schatzkammer Augusts des Starken. Von der Pretiosensammlung zum Grünen Gewölbe, Leipzig 1999, 23–24.

Wild, Klaus Eberhard: Zur Geschichte der Edelsteinbearbeitung. In: Im Strome sein, heißt, in der Fülle des Lebens stehen, Festschrift für Adolf Gruber, ed. Gymnasium Birkenfeld, Birkenfeld 1997, 341.

Page 94: REFLECTION AND RADIANCE OF
THE GODHEAD

Sources

Boodt, Anselmus Boetius de: Gemmarum
et lapidum historia, Hanau 1609,
Neudruck: Leiden 1647, Einleitung.

Secondary Literature

Bodesohn-Vogel, Inge: Zeittabelle. In:
Prag um 1600. Kunst und Kultur am
Hofe Rudolfs II., ed. R. J. W. Evans,
Joanaeth Spicer, Petra Kruse,
Freren/Emsland 1988, 15–26.
Chytil, K.: La Couronne de Rudolphe II,
Prag 1921, 17 ff.
Distelberger, Rudolf: Die Kunstkammer-
stücke. In: Prag um 1600. Kunst
und Kultur am Hofe Rudolfs II.,
ed. R. J. W. Evans, Joanaeth Spicer,
Petra Kruse, Freren/Emsland 1988,
457–460, 528–529.
Distelberger, Rudolf: Die Krone Kaiser
Rudolfs II., später Krone des
Kaisertums Österreich. In: Kunst-
historisches Museum. Weltliche
und Geistliche Schatzkammer,
Bildführer, 2. ed., Salzburg/Vienna
1991, 56.
Gonzalez-Palacios, A., Röttgen, S.:
catalog. In: The Art of Mosaics.
Selection from the Gilbert Collection,
Los Angeles County Museum of Art,
Los Angeles 1982, 83–84.
Krčálová, J., Piacenti, K., Aschengreen:
Castrucci. In: Dizionario biografico
degli italiani, vol. XXII, Rom 1979, 251.
Przyborowski, C.: Die Ausstattung der
Fürstenkapelle an der Basilika von
San Lorenzo in Florenz, Berlin 1982,
140.
Skřivánek, F. und M.: Die Familie
Miseroni und die Entwicklung ihres
Wappens. In: Adler, Zeitschrift für
Genealogie und Heraldik, vol. 13, 3,
1983, 65–79.
Weixlgärtner, A.: Die Weltliche Schatz-
kammer in Vienna. Neue Funde
und Forschungen. In: Jahrbuch der
Kunsthistorischen Sammlungen in
Vienna, vol. II., Vienna 1928, 296–297.
Zülch, W. K., Chytil, K.: Archivalische
Beiträge zu Hans Vermeyen und
Andreas Osenbruck, den Verfertigern
der österreichischen Kroninsignien.
In: Jahrbuch der Kunsthistorischen
Sammlungen in Vienna, vol. 3, Vienna
1929, 271 ff.

Page 96: THE EIGHTH WONDER
OF THE WORLD

Sources

Brief der Friederike Roltsch, der Kammer-
zofe der Großherzogin von Sachsen-
Weimar-Eisenach, an ihren geliebten
Albrecht am 13. August 1840.
quoted after: Enke, Paul: Bernstein-
zimmer-Report. Raub, Verschleppung
und Suche eines weltbekannten
Kunstwerkes, Berlin 1986, 46–47.
Grübel, Zacharias, Ortgies, Franz Herrmann: Correspondenz, Berlin,
5. Decembris 1716.
Konsalik, Heinz G.: Das Bernsteinzimmer,
Munich 1995, 535.

Secondary Literature

Bismarck, E. V.: Bernstein – das Gold
des Nordens, Wanderndes Museum
Schleswig-Holstein, 3, Neumünster
1972.
Heunisch, Carmen: Organische oder
biogene "Edelsteine". In: Faszination
Edelstein. Aus den Schatzkammern
der Welt. Mythos, Kunst, Wissenschaft, ed. Sybille Ebert-Schifferer,
Martina Harms, Darmstadt 1992,
41–51.
Kosmowska-Ceranowicz, B.: Über Bernstein. Osnabrücker naturwissen-
schaftliche Mitteilungen, vol. 17,
Osnabrück 1991, 21–24.
Krolewski, Wenjamin: Die Geschichte des
Bernsteinzimmers, Moskau 1966.
Schlee, D.: Bernstein-Raritäten, Staat-
liches Museum für Naturkunde,
Stuttgart 1980.
Weitschat, W.: Leben im Bernstein, Katalog
zur Sonderausstellung vom 10. März
bis zum 31. August 1978, Geologisch-
paläontologisches Institut der Univer-
sität Hamburg, Hamburg 1978.
Wermusch, Günter: Die Bernstein-Zimmer-
Saga. Spuren – Irrwege – Rätsel,
Munich/Berlin/Augsburg 1991.

Page 100: JEWELS AND TREASURES

Sources

quoted after: Syndram, Dirk (ed.): Das
Grüne Gewölbe zu Dresden. Führer
durch seine Geschichte und seine
Sammlungen, 2. ed., Munich 1997, 20.
quoted after: Syndram, Dirk: Die Schatzkammer Augusts des Starken. Von
der Pretiosensammlung zum Grünen
Gewölbe, Leipzig 1999, Umschlag.

quoted after: Vollstädt, Heiner, Lahl,
Bernd: Der Schneckenstein. In: Topas.
Das prachtvolle Mineral, der lebhafte
Edelstein, extraLapis No. 13, Munich
1997, 27.

Secondary Literature

Asche, Siegfried: Balthasar Permoser.
Leben und Werk, Berlin 1978, 178.
Quellmalz, Werner: Die edlen Steine
Sachsens, Leipzig, 1990, 5–189.
Syndram, Dirk (ed.): Das Grüne Gewölbe
zu Dresden, 2. ed., Munich 1997,
7–20.
Syndram, Dirk: Prunkstücke des
Grünen Gewölbes zu Dresden, 2. ed.,
Munich/Berlin 1997, 118–119.
Syndram, Dirk: Ein Denkmal für die
Kunst. Der Obeliscus Augustalis
im Grünen Gewölbe. In: Deutsche
Steineschneidekunst aus dem Grünen
Gewölbe zu Dresden, ed. Jutta
Kappel, Dresden 1998, 73–87.
Syndram, Dirk, Die Schatzkammer
Augusts des Starken. Von der Pre-
tiosensammlung zum Grünen
Gewölbe, Leipzig 1999, 22–26, 32.
Vollstädt, Heiner, Lahl, Bernd: Der
Schneckenstein. In: Topas. Das
prachtvolle Mineral, der lebhafte
Edelstein, extraLapis No. 13, Munich
1997, 26–37.

Page 104: THEFT, MURDER AND DEATH

Sources

Albertus Magnus: De mineralibus, ed.
Günther Goldschmidt, Basle 1983, 15.
Fee Mayrna-Tara: Der Diamant, die Dia-
mantin. In: Diamant. Der extreme
Edelstein, ed. Heinz Mahlzahn et al.,
Munich 2000, 5.
G. Plinius Secundus: Naturalis Historiae,
Liber XXXVII, Cap. XV, ed. Roderich
König, Zurich 1994, 46–49.

Secondary Literature

Glas, Maximilian: Von A-Z. Kurzge-
schichten berühmter Diamanten.
In: Kristallmuseum Riedenburg,
ed. Maximilian Glas, Brunswick 1980,
74–121.
Glas, Maximilian: Vajra, der geistige
Diamant. In: Diamant. Der extreme
Edelstein, ed. Heinz Mahlzahn et al.,
Munich 2000, 4–5.
Kristallmuseum Riedenburg (ed.): Das
Museum der Steine, die Geschichten
erzählen, Riedenburg 1998, 53–84.

Malzahn, Heinz: So bezwingt man die Härte 10. In: Diamant. Der extreme Edelstein, ed. Heinz Mahlzahn., Munich 2000, 68.

Malzahn, Heinz: Was ist ein Diamant eigentlich wert? In: Diamant. Der extreme Edelstein, ed. Heinz Mahlzahn et al., Munich 2000, 88.

Schmidt, Wolfgang: Kimberlit, Fahrstuhl oder Muttergestein. In: Diamant. Der extreme Edelstein, ed. Heinz Mahlzahn et al., Munich 2000, 50.

Vollstädt, Heiner: Die Geschichte der Diamantsynthese. In: Diamant. Der extreme Edelstein, ed. Heinz Mahlzahn et al., Munich 2000, 80.

Wild, Klaus Eberhard: Zur Geschichte der Edelsteinverarbeitung. In: Im Strome sein, heißt, in der Fülle des Lebens zu stehen, Festschrift Adolf Grub, ed. Gymnasium Birkenfeld, Birkenfeld 1997, 332, 341.

Woodward, Christine, Harding, Roger: Edelsteine, trans. Berthold Jäger, Markt Schwaben 1989/90, 25–27.

Page 108: IRIDESCENT WITH A HUNDRED LOVELY COLOURS

Sources

Goethe, Johann Wolfgang von: West-oestlicher Divan, ed. Joseph Kiermeier-Debre, Munich 1997, 11, 55, 133, 165.

Lessing, Gotthold Ephraim: Nathan der Weise, ed. Julius Petersen, Waldemar von Olshausen, Stuttgart 1979, 71–72, Vers 1913–1917.

Novalis: Heinrich von Ofterdingen (1802), Frankfurt am Main 1982, 64–65.

Poe, Edgar Allan: The Fall of House of Usher, trans. Arno Schmidt, Hans Wollschläger, vol. 2, Herrsching 1979, 650.

Poe, Edgar Allan: Das gesamte Werk in zehn Bänden, ed. Kuno Schumann, Hans Dieter Müller, vol. 9, Herrsching 1979, 41, 75, 83, 101, 121, 155.

Stifter, Adalbert: Bunte Steine. Erzählungen, ed. Helmut Bachmaier, Stuttgart 1994, 19–332

Secondary Literature

Jeter, Joseph Caroll: Adalbert Stifter's Bunte Steine. An Analysis of Theme, Style and Structure in Three Novellas, New York/Washington 1996, 23–179.

Pohl, Klaus-D.: Sinnbild neuen Lebens, Kristall und Kristallisation in der Kunst des 19. und 20. Jahrhunderts.

In: Faszination Edelstein. Aus den Schatzkammern der Welt. Mythos, Kunst, Wissenschaft, ed. Sybille Ebert-Schifferer, Martina Harms, Darmstadt 1992, 76–86.

Röder, S.: Höhlenfaszination in der Kunst um 1800. Ein Beitrag zur Ikonographie von Klassizismus und Romantik in Deutschland, Berlin 1985, 83.

Page 110: YOUR MAJESTY SHALL BE PLEASED

Sources

quoted after: Habsburg, Geza von: Fabergés Fama. In: Fabergé. Hofjuwelier des Zaren, ed. Geza von Habsburg, Munich 1986, 44–45.

Rapport du Jury International (Joaillerie), 1902, 371.

Walker, John: Self Portrait with Donors, quoted after: Forbes, Christopher: Von Fabergé fasziniertes Amerika. In: Fabergé. Hofjuwelier des Zaren, ed. Géza von Habsburg, Munich 1986, 101.

Secondary Literature

Bainbridge, Henry, C.: Peter Carl Fabergé, London 1949, Neudrucke: 1966 und 1974.

Forbes, Christopher: Fabergé, Die Firma und die Familie. In: Fabergé. Die kaiserlichen Prunkeier, ed. Christopher Forbes, Johann Georg Prinz von Hohenzollern, Irina Rodimtseva, Munich 1989, 15–20.

Forbes, Christopher: Von Fabergé fasziniertes Amerika. In: Fabergé. Hofjuwelier des Zaren, ed. Geza von Habsburg, Munich 1986, 100–103.

Habsburg, Geza von: Geschichte des Hauses Fabergé. In: Fabergé. Hofjuwelier des Zaren, ed. Geza von Habsburg, Munich 1986, 30–46.

Habsburg, Geza von: Fabergé als Steinschneider. In: Fabergé. Hofjuwelier des Zaren, ed. Geza von Habsburg, Munich 1986, 72–80.

Habsburg, Geza von: Fabergé und das Osterei. In: Fabergé. Hofjuwelier des Zaren, ed. Geza von Habsburg, Munich 1986, 92–99.

Hohenzollern, Prinz Johann Georg von: Die kaiserlichen Ostereier. In: Fabergé. Die kaiserlichen Prunkeier, ed. Christopher Forbes, Johann Georg Prinz von Hohenzollern, Irina Rodimtseva, Munich 1989, 7–13.

Snowman, A. Kenneth: The Art of Carl Fabergé, London 1953.

Solodkoff, Alexander von: Steinfiguren von Fabergé. In: Fabergé. Hofjuwelier des Zaren, ed. Geza von Habsburg, Munich 1986, 81–86.

Page 112: "LOOK ON ME AND SLUMBER"

Sources

Neruda, Pablo: El topacio, trans. Beatriz von Eidlitz. In: Mineral Digest, vol. 4, New York 1972.

Secondary Literature

Bernd-Klinger, Anita: Heilung durch Harmonie, Grafing 1992.

Bourgault, Luc: Ganzheitliche Edelsteintherapie. Wissen nach indianischer Tradition, Freiburg im Breisgau 1995.

Das große Lexikon der Heilsteine, Düfte und Kräuter, ed. Edition Methusalem, 7. ed., Neu-Ulm 1997, 10–279, 289–323.

Gienger, Michael, Newerla, Barbara, Schmidt, Jens: Mineralienkarten, Ludwigsburg 1994.

Gienger, Michael: Steinheilkunde, Saarbrücken 1995, 10 ff.

Gienger, Michael: Lexikon der Edelsteine. Vom Achat bis Zoisit, 2. ed., Fulda 1997, 14–573.

Glas, Maximilian: Kristallmuseum Riedenburg, Braunschweig 1990, 26–30.

Graf, Bernhard: Heilen mit Edelsteinen, 3. ed., Munich 2000, 12–21, 80–92.

Guhr, Andreas: Mythos der Steine. Macht und Magie, Hamburg 1995, 51–52.

Harder, Hermann: Lexikon der Minerale und Gesteine, Frankfurt am Main 1977.

Hochleitner, Rupert: GU Kompaß Edelsteine, Munich 1999.

Lindenberg, Christoph: Rudolf Steiner mit Selbstzeugnissen und Bilddokumenten, 6. ed., Reinbek bei Hamburg 1998, 104–109.

Markham, Ursula: Universelle Kräfte der Edelsteine, Munich 1997.

Martin, Katrin, Fröhling, Thomas: Katma-Edelsteinessenzen. 15 Edelsteinessenzen, ihr Wesen, ihre Wirkung, Munich 1997, 8–25.

Nassau, Kurt: Gemstone Enhancement, Oxford 1994.

Topas. Das prachtvolle Mineral, der lebhafte Edelstein. In: extraLapis No. 13, Munich 1997, 2–3.

Wimmenauer, Wolfhard: Zwischen Feuer und Wasser, Stuttgart 1992.

Index

Numbers in *italics* refer to pages with illustrations

© Prestel Verlag,
   Munich · London · New York, 2001

Front cover: Scarab pendant from Tutankhamun's grave, set with lapis lazuli,
turquoise and carnelian (p. 21)

Back cover: Pharaoh Tutankhamun's gold
mask (p. 18), Napoleon with the Regent
sword (p. 6/7), Rudolf II's imperial crown
(p. 95), Moor with Rock Emerals (p. 103),
Aztek mask (p. 87)

Endpapers: Lecture on precious stones in
the mineralogical book by the Franciscan
monk Bartholomaeus Anglicus, 1390/1400
(p. 79)

Frontispiece: Fine gems cut in classical
and unusual forms by Ekkehard F.
Schneider, Idar-Oberstein. Orange:
mandarin garnet; blue-green: tourmaline,
Namibia; blue: tanzanit, Tanzania; red:
tourmaline, Mozambique

Library of Congress Control Number:
2001094461

Prestel Verlag

Mandlstrasse 26 · 80802 Munich
Tel.: +49 (89) 381709-0
Fax: 49 (89) 381709-35

4 Bloomsbury Place · London WC1A 2QA
Tel.: +44 (20) 7323 5004
Fax: +44 (20) 7636 8004

175 Fifth Avenue, Suite 402 · New York,
NY 10010
Tel.: +1 (212) 995 2720
Fax: +1 (212) 995 2733

www.prestel.com

Translated from the German
by Paul Aston, Dorset; Mariana Schroeder,
Munich; Almuth Seebohm, Munich; and
Stephen Telfer, Edinburgh
Editorial direction by Christopher Wynne
Copy-edited by Danko Szabó

Design, typography, and production
by Heinz Ross, Munich
Font: Walbaum Antiqua
Cover design by Dorén and Köster, Berlin

Lithography by ReproLine, Munich
Printed and bound by Westermann Druck
Zwickau GmbH

Printed in Germany on acid-free paper

ISBN 3-7913-2581-7 (English edition)
ISBN 3-7913-2521-3 (German edition)

Picture credits